A Mystic's Journey to the Sacred Sites of France

Raylene Abbott

**Dedicated to my Mother and Father
who brought me into this sacred journey of life.**

TABLE OF CONTENTS

Introduction

One of the first memories of Sacred Pilgrimage I ever experienced was with my mother. We traveled and visited many of the California Missions, praying and lighting candles along our way. My mother gave me the gift of the way of prayer and devotions.

My connection with the Earth has been a lifetime love affair. Even as a small child my family would take vacations, exposing me to both the Sacred Sites of the Native American Indians and the beauty of nature. My dad would drive long hours on dirt roads and places hardly anyone else would travel and my mother would read the history of these place as we went along. These family vacations made lasting imprints inside of me of the places we visited.

One year I had read a book of Sacagawea, the Native American woman who was the guide for Lewis and Clark. That year my parents decided to take our vacation by following the Lewis and Clark Trail. Our journey ended at the gravesite of Sacagawea. I must have been all of 10 years old. As I stood standing in front of the grave of this Indian woman I was shedding tears. It was a powerful experience for someone so young. This was my first real experience of understanding the deeper meaning of pilgrimage.

When I was in my twenties, I worked and studied with a Native American Elder for ten years. He taught me about the secrets of the land and the natural altars that his people used for prayers and meditation. We traveled to many places in the wilderness together. This gave me an understanding of a natural earth pilgrimage. This trained me to open my eyes to a different understanding of the ways of nature and the Earth.

When I began to study Feng Shui, it opened up another facet within me. I began to understand how Feng Shui affected people's lives in both a positive or negative ways. This book is a portrayal of the various understandings I have developed over the years, but also expresses my own direct experiences and ancient memories of knowledge that has been forgotten.

Sacred Pilgrimage is both an inner and outer journey. It is designed to open us up to awakening and seeing life from a sacred point of view. A pilgrim may begin the journey because he or she is in need of a healing (such as a pilgrimage to Lourdes). However, what makes a journey sacred is the focus and intensity of a pilgrim's prayer, meditation and purpose.

Many people have come to France over the last few years looking for the lost secrets of Mary Magdalene, and exploring the possibility that her child may have started the Merovingian royal bloodline. At this point there is no written document that can prove such a claim and also the Merovingian kings were killed a long time ago. But the builders of the cathedrals, the Knights Templar, left clues and secrets in their Sacred Architecture.

The gnostics of the South of France, the Cathars, left their mark in the form of both castles and fortresses. But their fortresses did not protect them from the Albigensian Crusade. This crusade was started by the Catholic Church of Rome to wipe out the gnostic religion. The Cathars believed that direct experience with the Divine was far more important then the written word. What do the Merovingian Kings, the Knights Templar and Cathars all have in common? They all acknowledge Mary Magdalene as the Beloved of Christ and this was heresy for the Roman Catholic Church.

France is filled with these secrets. But many tourists come, visit and return home, without ever penetrating the depth of the Secrets of France. But beyond the esoteric secrets, the Sacred Sites of France still hold ancient power to answer prayers and bring healing to any sincere pilgrim.

The proper approach to a sacred site is the key that can decode the secrets and the truth that is hidden from the masses. I would like to make a few suggestions. Following them I have found deepens my experience when visiting sacred places.

Every Sacred Site has its own history and vibration. If you can understand the power of a particular site, then you can begin to understand how to align yourself with the site you are visiting. This book will be a guide to understanding both the vibration and also the Ley-Lines of the lands. It is very important to understand the power of the land that creates a Sacred Site.

You could also become aware of your inner process before you visit a site. I have found many times that when a particular issue within needs healing, it will arise the day or night before I visit the site. Because of this I usually pray or meditate the evening before. This prepares me for initiation.

I am very watchful for outer symbols along the way when I approach a site. When you arrive at your destination, take your time to really meditate and pray. Many times I have seen tourists come and go into the cathedrals without ever really sitting down and feeling and seeing what is really before them. It is through silent meditation and prayer that the Sacred will be revealed to you. It is more important to visit one place and have a deep experience of healing then visit a dozen places quickly and only walk away with a few photographs and no understanding of where you have been.

So I now would like to invite you to enter with me into the Mystical Journey of the Sacred Sites of this great nation we call France.

Raylene Abbott
Paris
June 6, 2010

Who is the Black Madonna and where did she come from?

Robert Graves writes: "The Black Goddess is so far hardly more than a word of hope whispered among the few who have served the apprenticeship to the White Goddess. She promises a new pacific bond between men and women... in which the patriarchal marriage bond will fade away... the Black Goddess has experienced good and evil, love and hate, truth and falsehood. She will lead man back to that sure instinct of love which he long ago forfeited by intellectual pride."

The fires of human experiences blacken the face of the Black Madonna: birth, death, love, sex, betrayal, joy and pain. She has walked through the lessons of human experiences and realized the essence of herself. She walks through the fire and comes out smiling for she has digested life's lessons fully. I am black but beautiful, it says in the Songs of Solomon, one of the most erotic love poems written between bride and the bridegroom. This was the Sacred Marriage between King Solomon and the Queen of Sheba.

The Black Madonna is a metamorphosis of different ancient goddesses: Isis, Cybele, Persephone, Ceres, Artemis of the Trees, Kali of India in the form of Parvati, the Mother Earth, Aphrodite, Bona Dea, known as the Good Goddess in Europe, Bridget and Vestia, the keeper of the sacred fires. Many of the Black Virgin sites are actually built on ancient Goddess temples.

Where have these statues come from?

Some of them have been brought back from the East during the time of the Crusades. Other statues have mysteriously been found when a field was plowed, or hidden in the hollow of a tree, or found in the blackberry brambles. Some statues have arrived in oarless boats, offering themselves freely to the town's people. Our Lady Guadalupe, also considered a Black Virgin, miraculously appeared on the robe of Juan Diego. She is called the Mother of the Americas. She has an offering shrine here in Paris in the Cathedral of Notre Dame.

Each holy site has its own story and often seems to be connected to the Ley-Lines, holy wells or fresh water springs, great mountains or dark, fertile forests. Saints down through the ages have used these sites to gather power and vision for their work. Joan of Arc of Orleans went to mass daily and prayed before a Black Madonna to gather strength before going into battle. St. Bernard had visions of drinking the milk from a Black Madonna breast. He was also known to be a great mystic, who also understood the secrets of nature.

Black Madonnas have been associated also with the cult of Mary Magdalene. It was she who was the Most Beloved of Christ and applied the balm before his death. She was the first to witness his resurrection.

The Knights Templar were keepers of the Black Madonna. She also has been associated with the Merovingian Kings of ancient France. There are over three hundred Black Madonna sites in France alone.

I have found by going on Sacred Pilgrimages we can find keys of understanding for our own life. These Sacred Sites are like living archetypes. They can bring wisdom, healing and revelation.

This year, my birthday fell upon a black moon and it seemed to be the perfect time for me to be on this pilgrimage. I welcome you through this doorway of time, history and sacred space to travel together as I share my journey, both inner and outer, through the Sacred Sites of France.

The Ley-Lines of France

The land of France is a wondrous tapestry of layered history. Where the great cathedrals stand today were once the sacred sites of the ancient tribe of the Gauls or temples from Roman times.

The Gauls and the Romans understood the natural magnetic earth currents, known as the Ley-Lines or *lignes telluric* in French. Feng Shui understands the importance of these magnetic earth currents for the placement in Sacred Architecture.

The Ley-Lines are found many times in rock ridges. If one looks closely into the face of these rocks one can begin to see the bodies of dragons. In Feng Shui this is called the Green Dragon Energy. The south of France has many examples of this: many villages are built beneath the power of the dragon. This is why there are so many stories of dragons in medieval folktales.

In China these types of ridges are called Lung-mei, Dragon Lines. They are invisible magnetic currents of energy that flow through the landscape. They create fertility for the Earth. There are always two main dragon lines: one is the yin line, representing the female polarity and the other the yang line,representing the male polarity. The male dragon line will be found in high, steep craggy ridges while the female line will be in softer areas in the landscape. But in both lines, if you look closely, you will see the body and shape of dragons.

The understanding of dragon lines was not only used in China. Other ancient cultures were also aware of them, such as in the British Isles, Australia, and the countries of Europe. The powerful magnetism experienced from these ley-lines caused the creation of many ancient roads, temples, standing stones and burial mounds.

The wildlife of the area also used such lines as their walking paths. Later on they were used for human foot traffic. Then the great road builders, the Romans, used the Ley-Lines to build their roads over the ley-lines.

The Gauls called the land between the main ley-lines the Wouivre. Wouivre means a snake that glides through the landscape. This magnetic serpent energy can also be connected to underground water currents or veins of gold, copper or silver. Sometimes it is also connected with different ridges in the landscape that have been pushed up by the magna deep in the earth. When this underground magnetic serpent energy surfaces, the land is fruitful. This ley-line power of the land was also used for initiations such as the Labyrinth of the Cathedral of Chartres. Walking the labyrinth of Chartres is an excellent example of how this serpent energy coils and rises from the center of the maze into the tower steeples of the church.

Mythology expresses the secrets of the Wouivre Currents when it portraits creatures such as Queen Melusine of the European folktales or the Naga beings of India. These mythical beings are half serpent and half women or are pictured as flying dragons and singing sirens.

These lines are a lot like acupuncture meridians in the human-body, but on a larger scale within the body of the Earth. The macrocosm is reflected in the microcosm. When Ley-Lines run straight across the land for many miles, it is considered bad Feng Shui, because the magnetic energy is unable to distribute the fertility throughout the land. Therefore, the ancients built temples or placed standing stones and burial mounds for the tribal chiefs to slow down the dragon's ley-line. In that way the fertility of the land could be distributed.

Menhirs are fertility stones. These stones sometimes are in the crypts of cathedrals or under the altar of a church. I discovered a Menhir under the altar of the church of Pignans in the South of France. One of these fertility stones was built into the wall at the church of Saint Marie de la Mer. This Menhir is shaped like a vulva. Gypsy women pray on this stone for the blessing of fertility so that they can have a baby, even to this today. In the crypt of Saint Victor's of Marseilles you will also find a Menhir in the shape of a dragon's head next to a stone relief of Mary Magdalene.

King's Tomb on the Ley-Line

Dolmens are another type of Standing Stone. These great stones are megalithic sanctuaries built by the ancients throughout Europe.

Stone dolmens also were used to collect the cosmic and magnetic energies of the ley-line currents. Dolmens were used for religious and ceremonial purposes, such as the standing stones of Stonehenge and France's Standing Stones of Montardier.

Dolmens were connected to the legends of the Goddess of the land who spun with magical distaffs, the dolmen being her distaff. There are different European legends that talk about the Goddess who carried her distaff, (dolmen stone) on her head or little finger. The Goddess spun her yarn while she walked from mountain to mountain, placing sacred stones along her way in a single night. The spinning Goddess is symbolic. She creates with the thread of spinning atoms that make up the matter of the material world. She has been known as Maya in India. However, she has many different names and forms in different cultures. Her weaving is the story of life on the material plane. She can be seen as Mother Earth expressing the infinite light of the formless into numerable forms found within nature. She spins and weaves so the story of life can be told. When she stops spinning the story and life, as we know it, ends.

Many of these spinning stories were later Christianized and merged into the stories of saints such as St. Radegonde who carried the standing stones of Poitiers. Mary Madeleine carried a dolmen to an island in the Vienne River. The Virgin of Aveyron carried dolmen stones in her apron as she was spinning. The cathedrals and churches were built around many of these stones. But when the stones were found in nature without the church they often were given the name of the devil, or witches tower or fairy rock to discourage people and to keep them away from the ancient memory of the land.

Sardinia, the island in Italy, tells the story of the witch Lughia Rajosa who lived amongst the standing stones. She spun with a magical distaff called Rocca fatata, the rocks of fate. She guarded the wealth of the land that took the form of thousands of jars of grains, oil, honey and herds of animals. Men would try to steel her wealth when she slept. Finally someone took her distaff and burnt it in an oven. She became so sad she wanted to cry but did not know how since she had never cried. Lughia transformed into thousands of insects known as the cicada. You can still hear the cry of the cicada reminding you of Lughia's loss of her magical distaff. The cicada is a sacred symbol here in the South of France. You can hear their song on warm nights during the spring and summer.

Even though this fairy tale comes from the island of Sardinia it still carries a thread of truth for all of us no matter where we live. A heavy veil has come between the Spirit of the Land and the people of the Earth. The Goddess's magical distaff was burnt just as many ancient records of the Sacred Feminine and women themselves were burned during the reign of church and selfish kings. Man used the wealth of the land without respecting the Laws of Mother Nature. The story of the Goddess of the land has been lost. The natural ley-line power of this Earth and its secrets were forgotten. The fertility of the land is dying in the climate of our modern world. The distaff of the Goddess of the Land has been broken and she is unable to spin her thread and precious few are able to hear her cries.

Many sacred sites of initiation around the world were built over these powerful Ley-Line grids. Some of the caretakers of these sites were priestesses and priests such as, the Snake Priestess of Crete, the Pharaoh and Queens of Egypt with their cobra crowns. There were the Druids of the Celt, with their serpentine jewelry and the Oracles of Delphi. They all used these grids as places for spiritual initiation. Their alignment with such power spots created initiates that could bring about healing, visions, speaking as oracles. They had many different spiritual gifts. We need to reawaken ourselves to the voice of Mother Nature, to initiation and, most importantly, to our Inner Self that remembers.

The Inner Ley-Lines

The true purpose of a Sacred Journey is to awaken one's consciousness. The outer journey is symbolic of the journey within. Just as the Earth has sacred Ley-Lines and power places, in the same way our own body also has its own Ley-Lines. When we align ourselves through prayer and meditation when visiting sacred sites, then initiations can take place. The energy for the great initiations are here if we approach a pilgrimage with the right attitude.

In the science of yoga they talk about the awakening of the Kundalini. The Kundalini energy is our sexual energy that has been raised up though the central channel. It is represented as two winged serpents. There are three specific subtle channels described as existing in our physical body. They are called *Ida* and *Pingala*. They coil around the central and most important channel, called Sushumna. When the Kundalini becomes activated through spiritual practice, the powerful force of the Kundalini moves up from the base of the initiate's spine and goes through the Sushumna channel.

However, there also exists a series of smaller channels in he body, called Nadis, or astral energy channels. Yoga teachings vary on how many there are, but generally suggest there are 72,000 energy channels.

When the Kundalini rises up through the major nadis, it is possible to experience blockages. These energetic blockages are connected to emotional traumas that have occurred in the course of the initiates' life, and also past lifetimes. When the Kundalini is truly activated these blockages get cleared and purified. The physical body can shake uncontrollably, strange sounds can be made to clear the throat chakra, the breathing becomes irregular and the body can move into spontaneous yoga postures. The Kundalini's purpose is to go through the central channel, clear through the blockages and activate all seven chakras. This initiation is not always easy. Unless a spiritual foundation of working with body, heart and mind has been prepared for this, one can have difficulties clearing these blockages in the nadis.

The dragon lines reflect the Earth's Kundalini with its two currents of Yin and Yang. The Ida and Pingala in the Kundalini System are reflected in the landscape by the two main dragon Ley-Lines. The subtler System of Wouivres, found between the two dragon Ley-Lines, represent the Earth's own Nadi System. The Naga Beings are the serpentine guardians of these Ley-Lines.

We can take this one step further by looking at earthquakes. They are a way that the Earth Kundalini is clearing out her own Nadi System. It is similar to the body uncontrollably shaking when the Kundalini passes through the blockages. The Earth at this time has absorbed many negative events and traumas of war, hate and greed that are in need of purification.

But the Kundalini Power of most people on this planet is dormant. This powerful spiritual initiation has been misunderstood down through history, starting with the myth of Adam and Eve and the serpent tempting Eve at the Tree of Knowledge. The Tree of Knowledge is the Central Channel of our Kundalini System. The serpent tempting Eve at the bottom of the tree is the dormant Kundalini, wanting to awakenand rise to the top of the crown chakra, the chakra of wisdom.

Many traditional roads to awakening do not involve the Kundalini opening. But I feel it is important to explain the truth about the serpentine Kundalini to clear up negative projections that have been placed on dragon and serpentine power that we often find in the Western Medieval archetypes.

Somehow the choice on this planet was to fall asleep in consciousness rather than to awaken, at least at that point of history and the times they are a-changing. The serpent became associated with evil and women associated with temptation. These are the hidden secrets of the ancient initiation sites I invite you on this journey of pilgrimage that pulls back the veil of time and the secrets that have been hidden within the churches and land of Europe.

Sacred Sites of Paris

There are so many sacred places here in Paris, filled with history and ancient memories. It could take a lifetime to discover them all. My purpose in this chapter is to reveal the hidden, and the esoteric sites that are not seen in your common tour guidebooks. I will share places that are off the beaten track of tourist sites. We will peel away the layers of lost memories found in sacred architecture, archetypes, symbols, and secret societies that left their mark on the city's planning. Paris is known as the City of Lights. It is one of the most beautiful cities in the world filled with mysteries waiting to be discovered.

\

Notre Dame of Paris and Pulling Back the Veils

The ancient name of Paris was Lutetia. A Celtic tribe lived there, called the Parisii. Then Rome conquered the city and it was renamed to Paris in the year of 212 A.D. This island of Lutetia was located in the river Sequana, which is now known as the River Seine.

What now is France was part of the Roman Empire. Their influence can still be felt in the history of the land. Isis was one of the deities that had been adopted by the Romans. That was the way of the Romans, they were tolerant of other Gods in the places they conquered. Even though the Isis myth came out of Egypt, she was worshipped throughout the ancient Roman Empire. Many temples in the Roman Empire were dedicated to Isis or Black Isis, an expression of the Goddess of Fertility

What now is Ile de la Cité was the island of Lutetia. Notre Dame is built in the middle of this island. The island itself is shaped like a boat. The Goddess Isis was known as a protector of sailors both by the Greeks and the Romans. And this may be why the Ile de la Cité came to be known as the Boat of Isis.

I begin this journey in front of the cathedral of Notre Dame at the Zero Point. The zero point is a brass stud. It is the geographical center, from where all the villages and cities of France are measured. Standing in the center of France, I contemplate not only the modern city around me, but also the layers of ancient history that exist beneath the island of Ile de la Cité.

The remains of a Roman ancient wall can still be found in the crypt of Notre Dame, built in the second century.

Note: The zero point in front of Notre Dame is a powerful place to close your eyes. Allow yourself to feel the ley-lines beneath your feet and don't forget to make a wish. It is also called the Center of the Rose Compass.

Falling Back in Time in Egypt

Isis Temple in Philae, Egypt

But let me take you back for one moment to the land of Egypt, to the island of Agila where the Temple of Isis now stands. This temple was moved between 1972 and 1980, piece by piece because the Aswan Dam was submerging the island of Philae.

I visited this sacred site this year, which became the last puzzle piece of my own sacred journey. I traveled to Egypt from France to join a group to visit the sites. We journeyed to Agila by small boats. When I stepped off the boat and glanced at my surroundings, the power of the Earth pulsed through my feet. A large out-cropping of rocks was before me. It looked like a giant dragon with a jeweled crown. I was in the very center of many ley-lines merging together. I was standing on Sacred Ground.

We walked onto the Temple Grounds where columns with the heads of the Goddess Hathor were before me. Many of these columns depicted Gods and Goddesses and offerings of great beauty. I am not an expert on the deeper studies of ancient Egypt. But I allowed myself to experience the inner realities by being available to the energy that is in such a Sacred Site. My feet trembled with anticipation. This was a place of ancient initiation. Philae was the center of Isis worship since 370 B.C. It was built by Napktnebef Kheperkare and expanded over the years by other rulers.

It was a place of pilgrimage during the Roman Empire. Both Greeks and Romans traveled here for healing. This place must have been the inspiration for the Romans to adopt the Goddess Isis as one of their major deities.

It was believed that Philae was the place that emerged from the primordial chaos. It was thought as the source of the Water of Life. The temple was built in the 30th Dynasty and was still in operation until the 6th century in spite of the arrival of Christianity. The Temple of Isis in Egypt was transformed in 535 AD and converted into a place of worship for the Christian Coptic Church until the coming of Islam. The Egyptians name for Isis was Ee-set. The Coptic pronunciation was Ese or Esi and the Greeks called her Isis. I find it interesting that this temple was submerged under water half of the year. Maybe the greater symbol of the temple being moved is about recovering something lost in the unconscious mind. Maybe the world is ready for the Revelation of Isis.

The worship of Isis is found throughout Europe in ancient temples, which are now the foundations of Medieval Cathedrals such as St Germain in Paris, Our Lady of Bon Port at the Côte d'Azur or Saintes-Maries-de-la-Mer that once was the ancient city of Ra here in the South of France.

It was time now for me to enter the doorway to the Temple. There is a Sacred Meaning of the Doorway into the Temple of Isis. "One side of the door is Yesterday. The other side is tomorrow. But the doorway you enter through is the NOW!"

We entered the NOW, as I stepped through the threshold, the Power of this place came crashing down from above through the top of my head into my body, with such force my knees began to buckle beneath me. I was taken over by the Holies of Holies, and by the Truth that lay behind the scene of such a place. People around me caught my arms. The Divine entered me. I had become hollow bamboo. I had come home.

It was if I was walking in a dream. My steps became light like as feather as we wove through the inner rooms of the Sanctuary of Isis. The ancient mythos of Isis is about finding the lost body parts of her dead husband Osiris. What is the deeper meaning of such a mystery? Do we not all feel separated in this world of matter? Do we not live in the illusion and it usually takes a crisis (Cry- Isis) in our lives to awaken and seek our wholeness? Isis recovers the lost parts of her spouse and makes him whole once again. Osiris was cut into fourteen body parts but Isis only found 13, because the penis of Osiris was missing, a hungry fish ate it. But Isis, being a mistress of alchemy, fashioned a penis from lapis lazuli. She then impregnated herself and gave birth to the falcon-headed God Horus, the falcon having the power of a higher view.

The Egyptian obelisk is the grand symbol of the phallus of Osiris that was created by Isis. We can find this symbol at the Place de la Concorde, here in Paris. This particular obelisk stands in direct alignment with the Church of Mary Magdalene, located only several hundred yards distant.

We then entered the birth room of the Isis Temple in Philae. The walls were darkened by time and age but there before me was a relief of Isis suckling the child Horus. What was I being asked at this time in my life to bring to birth? Nothing more or less than my SELF.

The group moved through the different rooms in the temple, but then we were taken to the shrine room. This is where the Altar of Isis still stands. This altar once housed a granite cupboard that held the statue of Isis to which offerings were given every day. Once a week the statue was placed on a barge that crossed to the island of Bigen to visit the tomb of her spouse Osiris. This cupboard that once housed the statue of Isis now is found in the Louvre here in Paris.

Many Egyptian artifacts were brought back to France by Napoleon. Napoleon himself had initiations in the Great Pyramid of Giza, one of the Greatest Initiations sites known to man. And maybe these initiations brought the lessons of failure to Napoleon. The soul may have needed to learn the lesson that the greatest thing one could ever conquer is one's own self.

Our small group gathered around the altar of Isis. We placed our hands on the stone slab. The energy was more then my body could bear. It came through my feet into my hands like electricity wanting an outlet. My mind deepened into prayer for those around me, prayer for the world, and prayer for those who needed healing. Prayer and love was the only thing I could feel. Those around me supported my body. I abandoned myself to what unavoidably wanted to be expressed. It did not matter if people around me accepted or rejected me. There was nothing I could do but surrender to what was unfolding. I was ushered out of the altar room; my feet felt like they were gliding on air. A friend had my arm as my strong and silent protector. I heard women walking by in the crowds hissing like snakes. A long time ago, priestesses of Isis would repeat her name, emphasizing the last syllable like the hissing of a snake the sacred sound of Mother Kundalini.

Silence entered me, intermingled with prayer. I was in the fresh and open air - not in this world and not of it either.

Back in Modern Day Paris

I find myself standing in front of Notre Dame, looking at the famous western rose window. I silently begin to say a mantra to Isis. Isis La Déesse (Goddess Isis). This is how I begin my sacred journey on the Ile de La Cité, which represents the Boat of Isis.

I look up at the 28 stone statues of the Kings of Judah. They were built into the face of the cathedral. What is interesting is that in the bible there is only the mention of 19 kings. Twenty-eight kings represent the 28-day lunar cycle of the Moon Goddess. The western rose window is symbolic of the womb of the Great Goddess herself. Stone reliefs make up a living book of Hermetic knowledge.

When you walk through the door of Notre Dame there you can see a stone relief of a bishop holding a shepherd hook. He seems to be stepping on a dragon. But if one takes a second look one realizes that the dragon is actually curling up the bishop's staff. The dragon is the spiritual power of the Earth Mother's Kundalini, rising from the ley-lines of this Sacred Site. The bishop's shepherd hook is not much different from the Pharaoh hook of ancient Egypt that was used to rule his people.

Once I enter the cathedral, I move through the crowds of tourist. I light a candle for a friend's mother who recently died. I sit in silent meditation. Sitting next to me is a beautiful black woman. She was in deep silence. We are sitting in silence together before a multitude of flickering candle lights. We are praying before a statue of Virgin and Child. This statue is better known as Our Lady of Paris.

Many tourists are moving through the crowd completely unconscious that this is a place of prayer. In spite of this we continue our meditations. When I stand up to leave, the black woman and myself make eyes contact. We meet each other soul-to-soul. I feel the Black Madonna archetype is embodied in this woman before me. Her eyes are soulful. There is an impression of sweet sadness, as she looks deep into my eyes. I am open and receptive. For a brief moment our souls are in communion. Then I rise and make my way through the cathedral.

I come to the Chapel of Mary Magdalene. A heavy black curtain drapes this chapel so that I have to poke my head around the curtain to see the image of Magdalene painted on the wall. She is washing the feet of Christ and above her stands Judas with his bag of silver that hangs from his belt. What is interesting about this picture that the bag of money is resting on the back of Mary Magdalene.

Historically speaking this event is a subject of considerable debate of who this woman might be since in one of the gospels she was addressed as only Mary. But it was Judas who complained of wasting the costly scented balm on the feet of the Master. This anointing of costly spikenard was one of the rituals of a Temple Priestess of the Goddess to initiate a Sacred King who was doomed to die for the good of his people. The matriarchal line of queens had the power to initiate men to become kings. Jesus replied to Judas that Mary was anointing him for his burial. This was an ancient agriculture rite. When the land was not in prosperity and harvests were bad they gave the life of the King as an offering. Christ was giving his consent to sacrifice himself for such an act. This gives a whole other picture on who Christ might have been and the role Mary Magdalene.

It was in the bible in the Gospel of Mark 16:9 that talks about Christ casting out the seven devils out of Mary Magdalene. What may have looked like an exorcism to the un-initiated could have been the initiation of the Kundalini moving through Mary Magdalene's body opening and awakening the seven chakras. This type of initiation comes with rolling around on the ground violent movements through the body and many strange manifestations.

The Temple Priestess of Isis knew the initiations of Kundalini awakening. The worship of the cobra was the symbol of those initiations. The archaeologists have found hieroglyphics of cobras in the ancient temples dedicated to the Goddess Isis. The archetype of the Goddess Isis is like an over lay of the story of Christ and Magdalene. The saints of the Catholic Church seemed to have absorbed the ancient myths of the Goddess so that the new religion was easier to sell to the pagans. And if that did not work there was always the Inquisition.

I make my way through the church to leave. I gaze up at the ceilings before me. The sacred architecture of the arch ceiling gives you the feeling of going through a giant birth canal. I walk through the main exit of Notre Dame and I begin to study the stone reliefs on the outside of the face of the church. There are three stone images that are next to each other. One image on the stone is Magdalene, holding her alabaster jar. The other two images are a crayfish and Christ holding the sacrificial lamb.

I remember seeing some of these same images on The Marseille Tarot. This older Tarot deck has been known to hide the hidden knowledge of Mary Magdalene. This Tarot Deck surfaced in southern France in the years after the dissolution of the Knights Templar in 1307. The Knights Templar were the mystical architects of the medieval cathedrals. They were known to have honored the Sacred Feminine. This was the reason for their building so many churches to the Virgin Mary. The Sacred Feminine was honored and upheld symbolically throughout their medieval designs.

The Church and King Philippe of France condemned the Templars as heretics. King Philippe at the time had a cash flow problem and since the Templars controlled the bank system of Europe it became an easy way for Philippe to end his troubles. If the Templars could be condemned as heretics, then all their properties could be divided by church and state, leaving both the King and the Church rich. But not all the Templars were caught. Some escaped to Italy, the Pyrenees, and also Scotland.

Some of the Knights believed that Mary Magdalene was the wife of Jesus Christ. Tarot decks began to surface in Italy that carried the heresy symbols of the lost feminine. The Italian Tarot decks began to travel to France into the city of Marseille. I believe a great deal of heretical symbology is hidden in the older tarot decks of this time. I think that the Moon card of this Tarot deck was depicting the Templars own beliefs of the Magdalene being the bride of Christ.

Going Through the Back Door of Notre Dame

We are in the front of Notre Dame, looking at the left door of the Cathedral. Next to the door I see a stone relief with a crayfish. The crayfish on the stone relief is like the crayfish on the Moon Card of the Tarot. We also should take into consideration that the face of this wall of Notre Dame represents the Lunar Great Goddess. The crayfish in the tarot is hiding in the depths of the water. It cannot leave its watery domain since there are two fierce dogs in front of the water. The upper part of the card is a picture of the Moon, eclipsing over the Sun. This eclipse is the marriage of the **Solar and the Lunar** or better known as the **Hieros Gamos** or Sacred Marriage. In the background of this card there are two towers. When I first saw this card I realized the heresy behind the images.

The crayfish is really the older image of the crab. The crab is the astrological symbol of Cancer. Cancer is the sign of the **Great Mother, the Lunar Goddess**. The crayfish is hiding in the depths of the water, afraid to come out. The crayfish's body is also shaped like a man's penis. Do you remember Osiris who lost his penis because of a fish had eaten it? This penis looking crayfish represents the union of both the sacred male and the sacred female.

The lunar eclipse that symbolizes the Sacred Marriage is the marriage between the priestess queen with the sacred king. The two towers in the distance also have meaning. The name Magdalene means tower. There are two towers! The dogs are symbolic of both of the Catholic Church and the political powers of the King.

The Great Mother is none other than Great Goddess Isis. And her priestess queen is Mary Magdalene. The Sacred Marriage is of Christ and the Magdalene. But the truth of this story could not be revealed openly because of the Catholic Church and the politics. The crayfish image on the stone relief was a way to reveal the truth of Christ's story if one understood what the symbols meant. The Marseille Tarot was a decoding system for those who had been initiated into the great secrets. Since so many of the original architects of the cathedrals who placed these heresy symbols into the church were murdered, the tarot was a way to keep the information alive in Europe disguised as a common card game.

The other stone relief is Christ holding the sacrificial lamb. But what was really being sacrificed? How many people have been sacrificed to hide the truth? The traditional meaning of the Moon card is deceit or hidden knowledge. It is very interesting what can be seen on the walls of Notre Dame.

I now make my way around the island of Ile de la Cité. It is a pleasant walk with many beautiful sites along the way. When I am on Sacred Journey I like to keep my mind on a spiritual focus. So I continue to silently recite a mantra with each step.

I arrive at the tip of the island, which represents the helm of the boat of Isis. The island is in the River Seine. There is an open gate to a small garden called Square de I'Ile-de-la-Cité and the Memorial des Martyrs de la Deportation. This place became a memorial to 200,000 French Jews that have met their deaths in Nazi concentration camps. The memorial is underground, housing the names of all those who died. It is interesting to note that a memorial of this tragedy has been placed at the helm of the boat of Isis. Those in power understood that he who controlled the helm of the ship of Ile de la cité of Paris ruled the land. The Nazis knew this and set up headquarters in the center of the island during their occupation of France in WW II.

I offer flowers and continue on my walk, saying silent prayers for all those who lost their lives and their families during this war.

My sacred walk brings me to the other end of the island, called Pont Neuf. This would be the symbol of the stern of Isis's boat. This is the Square of du Vert Galant. This park has been named after King Henry IV. This is where the Grand Master of the Knight Templars, Jacques de Molay, was burnt at the stake in the year of 1314 for heresy. According to the myth, the compassion of Queen Isis carries the souls who have died to the afterlife in her Solar Boat. Ile de la cité of Paris represents the boat of Isis.

I continue around the island to where the Sainte-Chapelle resides. King Louis IV, who later was ordained as a saint, built the small medieval chapel. The purpose of this chapel was to house the relics of Christ. The crown of thorns and part of the Holy Spear were displayed in this chapel in the year 1239. It was said that he who possess the Holy Spear of Christ rules the world. Rudolf Steiner writes about this is his book the "Spear of Destiny". The relics of Christ are no longer in Sainte-Chapelle. But what remains is an ancient architecture that is a true jewel of Paris. The first floor is painted in deep blue with thousands of small golden Fleurs de Lis, decorating the wall. The fleur de lis was the sign of royalty, but its more esoteric meaning was the womb of Mary Magdalene. It also was interpreted to be the womb of the Virgin Mary.

I walk up a narrow stone staircase to the second floor. There were the most spectacular stain glass windows of Europe. Stories from the bible are told throughout many small windows that create a living book of color and light.

I slowly walk down the central aisle of the chapel, silently saying my mantra. Both sides of the church are lined with tourists. I look down at my feet and I am standing on large Fleurs de Lis embedded into the floor. I slowly approach the altar and find myself transported into another time and space. My dress becomes blue velvet, trailing behind me as I walk. I feel as if I am part of the royal lineage and I remember when the relics of Christ actually here housed in this church. All of this happens in a flash of understanding and suddenly I find myself back again in present day. Silently I am continuing to say the Mantra of Isis.

I now have returned to the back garden of Notre Dame and from where I stand I can see a bridge that connects the island of Ile de la cité with the island of Ile de Saint Louis. The island of Isis joined with the island of the old king of France. Louis understood the marriage of the Goddess and the King would ensure his power on the throne, therefore the symbols were wedded in the layout of the city of Paris.

I returned to my walking meditation and now through my silent steps I too bridge Goddess Isis with the island of King Saint Louis.

The streets of Saint Louis are lined with many boutiques. You can find the finest perfumes, foie gras, an old-fashioned marionette store and fashionable hats.

At the end of the main street my interest is drawn to a small church of Saint Louis. This church contains a modern day image of the Black Virgin. But it is a statue of Saint Anne, grandmother of Christ that catches my eye. This statue of Saint Anne looks like what they call here in France the icons of Bonne Mere, the Good Mother. These particular types of statues look more like a Fairy Godmother who will grant your wishes. The face on the statue of Saint Anne is gentle, kind and smiling with almost a twinkle in her eye if you could imagine a twinkle on a wooden statue. It is one of my favorite icons. Her Presence is so happy. If she does not hear your prayer she surely will grant your wish. The name Ann was a title of a temple priestess throughout the Middle East and the Mediterranean. They also used the name Anu, or Anna. (Do not go to this church during lunch hours or you will find the doors closed.)

I leave the church and walk along the outer quiet streets of the island, coming back to full circle at the connecting bridge of the two islands. It is a bit of a walk but it is well worth the journey. When you take this walk with a sacred intention you will be joining the Sacred Feminine and Sacred Masculine of Paris together and also deep inside of yourself.

Modern Day Interpretation of the Myth of Isis

Even though the myth of Isis and Osiris originates in ancient Egypt, the story has much to teach us in our present world.

The Romans refer to Queen Isis, the Egyptian Goddess, as *She of One Thousand Names*. Isis has been given many titles over the course of history. Many of Isis's identities were absorbed into the Cult of the Virgin Mary. The following list contains a few titles of the Goddess Isis:

She Who Knows How to Make Right Use of the Heart
Mother of Heaven
Mother of the Gods
The One Who is All
The Lady of the Green Crop
Star of the Sea
The Brilliant One in the Sky (this refers to constellation Virgo)
Moon Shining Over the Sea
Great Lady of Magic
Light Giver of Heaven
Lady of Words of Power
Lady of Abundance
Lady of Bread
Lady of the Waves
The Throne
Lady of Sekhmet
Giver of Life
Lady of Philae
Lady of the Countries of the South

The God Mother

The myth of Isis is symbolic on many different levels. Isis's spiritual quest is to reunite with her husband Osiris. Our own spiritual journey guides us to uniting with our inner male and female.

The crisis of Isis is finding all the missing pieces of Osiris. Our spiritual journey often starts from a crisis (Cry Isis) in life. Our disappointments and suffering can be the first steps that bring us unto our spiritual quest. Isis is the Great Mother. Her veils represent the illusionary form of the material plane. It is the world of form. She is the goddess of the 13 moons. Her moon cycle teaches us how life is in physical form. Life has a beginning symbolic of the new moon. It has a flowering symbolic of the full moon. Life also has a destructive cycle that is represented by the waning moon.

Isis has a magical moon mirror that gives her the powers to reflect on these three aspects of life. It also lets her see the inner light in everyone and every life experience. When Isis has this type of understanding, she exists in the knowing that all circumstances are ever changing. This is the spiritual journey that helps us find our true essence. Osiris, husband and brother of Isis, is symbolic of the Infinite Light that is hidden in all things. This is why it is so important for Isis to reassemble Osiris. It is essential to return to the view of wholeness, to reestablish the holiness of our life without looking through the lens of separation.

The mystical boat of Isis travels down the Great River Nile. The boat is her vehicle to find the missing pieces of Osiris. Our bodies are the vehicles we are given in life to begin the journey of finding our True Self. Our physical vehicle is subjected to the three phases of the moon and the temporary conditions in this material world. Our bodies are also subjected to the genetical conditioning we inherit from our family line. Isis wears the red belt with a knot. This red belt is the symbol of our bloodlines.

The boat travels down the River Nile. The River Nile is symbolic of the Central Channel that the Kundalini moves through. Isis is also the serpent Queen symbolized by her golden serpentine crown. The Kundalini, the sleeping serpent that lays dormant at the base of the spine, is waiting to reveal itself. When this serpent is awakened it raises through the Central Channel, initiating and revealing the mysteries. The River Nile was the symbol of the Central Channel and the upper and lower Egypt represented the higher and the lower chakras. The temple sites that are still on the River Nile were the ancient initiation sites of those different chakras we all have in our bodies wanting to be awakened.

Just as Isis finds the missing pieces of her beloved, we also need to find the missing pieces of ourselves. Isis is the form of matter we see in this world. Osiris is the Infinite Light. He is the Christ Light that lives in everything. Isis resurrects him. The two lovers of this myth are the Union of Matter and Spirit or Form and Emptiness, as the Buddhists would say. The myth of Isis and Osiris is the ancient foundation of the Jesus and Magdalene story. You may remember that Jesus as a baby fled to Egypt with his mother and father. Most likely he was trained in the Egyptian mysteries and was well aware of the ways of Goddess Isis. The Black Madonnas of France hold the secrets of Isis in the form of the Virgin Mary waiting to be discovered.

Directions:
Notre Dame: 10 Rue du Cloitre-Notre Dame Metro Cite
Sainte Chapelle: 4 Blvd. Palais de Justice
The Church of St. Louis-en-l'Ile: 19 Bis Rue St Louis-en-I'lle Metro Pont Marie
Memorial des Martyrs et de la Deportation: Square de I'll-de-la-Cité
Square du Vert-Galant: Pont Neuf, Metro Pont Neuf

Roman Prayer to Isis by Apuleius

O Holy, Blessed Lady,
Constant comfort to humankind,
Whose beneficence and kindness nourishes us all.
And whose care for those in trouble is as a loving Mother.
Who cares for all Her children - You are there when we call.
Stretching out Your Hand to put aside that which is harmful to us,
Untangling the web of Fate in which we may be caught,
Even stopping the stars if they form a harmful pattern.
All other deities, whether bountiful or merciless,
Do reverence to Thee.
It is Isis who rules the world, stamping out the powers of evil,
Arranging the stars to give us answers, causing the seasons to come
and go.
Commanding the wind to move ships,
Giving the clouds to water the growing seeds,
So that we may have food.
If I had one thousand mouths,
And one thousand tongues within each,
Still I could not do justice to Your Majesty.
Yet I will forever remember Your Help in my time of need.
And I will keep Your Blessed, Sacred image
Deep within my heart forever.

Notre Dame des Aires

There is a very interesting little chapel right outside of Paris called Notre Dame des Aires, Our Lady of Air. What makes this chapel different from many sites I have seen here in France is the bronze statue of the Virgin Mary. This statue holds her hands high up into the air, reminding us of the position of the Ancient Goddess who is drawing down the powers of the Cosmos to bring Divine Blessings to the Earth. We see this position in the older archetype of the Winged Isis. The ancient Egyptians invoked Isis, "Mistress of the Gods, Thou bearer of wings." She is invoked again by calling, "The Living Souls who are in their hidden places praise the mysteries of thee, O Thou who art their Mother, Thou the source from which they sprang, Thou who makest for them a place in the hidden."

We see the memory of the archetype of Isis in our Notre Dame des Aires. This chapel was built at the turn of the 19th century to bless early aviators of Paris. I do not think this statue was built with the hidden meaning of Isis in mind, but I find it is interesting that her presence remains in the unconscious mind of artist. And then again, maybe it was not unconscious.

Direction
From La Defense take the L train towards Saint Cloud and get off at Val d'Or. You can see the church from the station. The church is rarely open except on Sundays during mass.

Shaking a Leg on the Ley-Lines of Paris

Dragon Tree at the River Seine

Paris is a place of ancient initiations and mystical adepts. Many of the old initiation sites are built over underground streams. Where there is underground water there are ley-lines. Gargoyles are found on top of the Gothic cathedrals. Their presence is a sure sign that the ley-line energies are near. Gargoyles are associated with an old French legend about one of the chancellors of the Merovingian Kings, St.Romaus. The legend goes there was a giant dragon, whose name was Gargouille. Gargouille the dragon ravaged the countryside, bringing disease and havoc wherever he went.

Nobody in their right mind would fight the dragon except St. Romaus and one condemned prisoner who had been sentenced to death. It is said that St. Romaus made the sign of the cross and the dragon became tamed. The saint then brought the dragon back in front of the church and threw him on a fire, but his head would not burn. Then Saint Romaus placed Gargouille's head on top of the church where it ever remained.

Every legend has a small thread of truth one can find if we look closely. The old records about sacred architecture and the ley of the land were most likely burned or hidden by the Catholic Church. Those texts were filled with knowledge of the power of true initiation. The Knights Templar, who were condemned prisoner themselves, held the secret understanding of working with the Ley-Lines. They also meet their death by burning. One master mason could hold thousands of secrets of Sacred Architecture.

St. Romaus was also a Catholic Bishop of Rouen. It was St. Romaus, a man of the church, who wanted to burn the dragon. Maybe the burning of the dragon by Bishop St. Romaus hinted at the truth that had been hidden. The dragon was burned and so were the keepers of this hidden knowledge, the Knight Templars. The head of the dragon could not be destroyed because secrets are still in the walls of the architecture of the cathedral, for those who have the eyes to see.

Dragons on the top of temples are traditionally found in the East to not only protect the temple but also to funnel the Ley-Line energy up the walls of the temple.

The Knights Templar traveled throughout the mid-east during the time of the Crusades. They were exposed to many different architectural designs, mathematics, different religions and even great secrets we do not even understand today. The Templars created rainwater gutters in their designs of the Gothic cathedrals to protect the architecture from water damage. The end of each rain gutter became a face of a gargoyle. The ancient Egyptians were the first to create rain gutters to direct water off the roofs of their buildings.

You will find the Gargoyles guarding many of the Gothic Churches of France. Notre Dame is famous for their Gargoyles but just a short walk away is the Latin Quarter. There you can find one of the best displays of Gargoyles on the church of St. Severin. St. Severin is a small Gothic church and because it does not have the towering rooftops as Notre Dame it becomes very easy to photograph these strange creatures on the church. The Gargoyles grotesque appearance was used to scare away any evil spirits that might bother a sacred site.

Directions: 1 Rue des Pretres, 75005 Metro San Michel and Cluny la Sorbonne

Saint Clothide

As I was visiting the churches of Paris, I came across an image of St. Prudentia in Sainte Clothilde. Her appearance was more like a priestess of the Goddess than a saint. According to the Church, St. Prudentia was one of the early Roman martyrs. She was said to be a pupil of St. Peter, a Roman Virgin and she spent her time baptizing Pagans. Her body was found in the catacombs in Salaria. It more likely she was a priestess from the Goddess Temple. The Church needed to attract pagans to the new faith. Turning the priestess into a saint was a way to do this.

The picture of St. Prudentia had an image of a serpent on her right and a beehive on her left. The beehive was an ancient symbol of the Goddess Venus. The priestesses of Venus were called Melissa. The serpent had been used as the symbol of the Goddess long before the story in the bible of Adam of Eve. The Adam and Eve story represents dualism, good and evil, black and white. But the symbol of the serpent was really about transformation. That transformation was about one's own inner negative emotions that have been held in the body. This may be why Prudentia was represented with the rites of baptism, for water is the symbol of cleansing of the emotions.

I also came across St. Prudentia in the Church of St. Louis, which I found in the back of the Church. In this image she held both a snake in her hand and a mirror. The mirror is an important symbol. It represents the need for self-reflection. Our negative emotional memories are found in the belly. These unconscious memories are asking to be transformed. When this is done, the serpent becomes the healing staff of Caduceus, which is the medical symbol of doctors even today.

This image of Prudentia in the church also showed a bucket of eggs. Eggs were the symbol in pagan times for fertility. The temples of the Goddess were very connected to the Ley-Lines and the blessing of the fertility of the land. A bottle of wine was there that appeared to be an offering for the serpent in the picture.

There is a problem with the story of Adam and Eve and that is the evils of this world were projected outside oneself on to woman. And women have suffered for this ever since. When true initiation happens, one begins to understand that we hold negative emotions in our bellies. We realize we need to become responsible for our own emotions and start the process to transform them. When we have the courage to cease our projections on to others, be that women, different cultures or religions, then real transformation can happen.

The symbol of the serpent is the power of the Kundalini. It is the sleeping sexual energy at the base of the spine. When this energy is awakened, its raw power runs through the spine, initiating all seven chakras. Kundalini is the sexual power awakened that is used for the initiate's enlightenment process. This initiation can feel like a freight train running through your living room and it takes a solid spiritual understanding to go through such initiation gracefully. Kundalini is also about waking up your spiritual power.

But when this power has not been completely dedicated to the Divine, it can become corrupted with human will and human ego. Then something that might have been used to awaken could turn into a power trip. I am sure this was one problem that happened within the Goddess Temples because of the human condition. And it might have been the reason many of these ancient secrets were concealed from the masses. Maybe the true message of Prudentia is to have prudence and humbleness when such initiations take place.

Note: The bee symbol also had been used by Napoleon. Napoleon was known to have turned some of the Catholic Churches during his time into Pagan Temples, including Notre Dame.

Dream Time: The night before visiting this church I had a dream. I dreamed I was holding a live serpent. My right hand was over the left side of my pelvis, holding its tail. And my left hand was over my heart, holding the serpent's head. The serpent felt like a very strong electrical currant running though my hands. The electrical current felt as if it was coming out the center of my heart. I woke up with my hands in this position. I was fully awake, still experiencing the electrical current running though my hands and in my heart. It felt like holding the ancient healing wand. Something you might see a priestess hold or The Winged God Mercury. There is an old well behind our apartment building, reminding me that I am living over an underground water source. Where there is underground water there are Ley-Lines.

Directions: 12 Rue Martignac Metro Solferino, Varenne, Invalides

Saint Germain des Pres

The first time I visited Paris was in the January of 2000. We had not even been in the city for over an hour when we began to explore one of the oldest Churches of Paris, St Germain des Pres on the Left Bank. It is a 6th century church built in the year 542 by King Childbert. King Childbert was part of the lineage of the Merovingian Kings. There are Merovingian Kings buried in this old Romanesque style cathedral. But this church also has ancient history since it was once the temple of the Black Goddess Isis. There once had been a statue of Black Isis in this church until the Bishop Guilaume Briconnet destroyed the statue in the year 1514. The Church also has a history of witch burning in front of Saint Germain during the time of the Inquisition.

The first time I went into Saint Germain des Pres I passed through its door, offering one of the beggars a coin for his can. Giving coins to one gypsy when I go out on such adventure has become a little tradition for me here in Paris. I see it as a little offering to open the doors of magic for me here in the city. I usually have a few coins in my pocket for such occasion so I don't have to open my wallet. Ah, Paris does have those moments that are truly magical and mystical like no other city I have ever visited.

I enter the church and in the corner there are many taper candles all a-flame, placed around the statue of the Blessed Virgin. I light a candle make a prayer and then move to a chapel where an icon of Saint Theresa the little flower stands. St. Theresa is the saint that grants small favors. The energy began to intensify inside of me. I begin to shake as the Kundalini rises from Earth to Sky through my body. Just in that moment a woman breaks out in song; she is singing Ave Maria. Tears are pouring down my face. My heart is completely open to the experience. The song stops, my body becomes calm again and I hear an inner voice in my heart saying, *welcome home my daughter*.

A few years ago a very old statue of the Virgin Mary was found here in Paris. This ancient statue is now in the back of the cathedral. It is not like any other statue of the Virgin I have ever seen. It now has become an icon for the devotions to the Blessed Mother in Saint Germain des Pres. I returned to the Church and to find a group of people singing Medieval Praises to the Mother. The quality of the voices of this group, combined with the ancient beauty of this icon, brought me to a deep Inner Silence and a Peace beyond words. This moment reminded me of one of the hundreds of names of the Virgin Mary, one of her titles being The Queen of Peace.

Directions: 3 Pl Saint Germain des Pres, 75006 Metro St. Germain des Pres

Saint Sulpice

The church of Saint Sulpice gained additional fame here in Paris because of the movie *The Da Vinci Code*. The zero meridian starts at St Sulpice. This meridian was the first creation of the longitude and latitude lines before the use of Greenwich time. There is a line that runs through this cathedral made from brass. This line is also known as the Rose-Line. It is said that the Rose-Line is symbolic of the royal bloodline of the Merovingian Kings. The old legends claimed that the Merovingian Kings were from the bloodline of Mary Magdalene and Christ. This Rose-Line that runs through Saint Sulpice also travels down through Southern

France and runs through Rennes-le-Chateau. There has been so much written on Rennes-le-Chateau by many different sources. But to make a long story short, a priest at Rennes-le-Chateau by the name of François Bérenger Saunière found a secret document in a pillar in his church. He went to the bishop of Carcassone, who directed him to go to Saint Sulpice in Paris. When he returned from Paris, the priest had access to large sums of money that seemed to come from out of nowhere. There are many theories on the connection of Rennes-le-Chateau and Saint Sulpice.

But what is there also in Saint Sulpice is a large gnomon. Gnomon is the Greek word for sundial. The sundial of St. Sulpice runs north to south. This gnomon was used to calculate the dates of Easter or other sacred days that change year from year with the movement of the sun. Charles Le Monnier made the sundial in the year of 1743. It was created as an accurate way to set clocks by. You can see the Rose-Line run through the sundial itself and then go through the church. The Rose-Line may have been inspired by another document of esoteric knowledge that is called the "Red Serpent." This document is now in the Bibliothèque Nationale. This document is from the "Dossiers secrets." It contains the lineage names of the Merovingian Kings. The "Dossiers secrets" also contains the building plans of Saint Sulpice.

It also contains eulogy poems to "Isis Queen of all Sources Benevolent." The Red Serpent is known also as the Red Girdle, sometimes called the Red Belt of Isis. One title of the Goddess Isis is "Isis the Queen of Crowns of the North and South," like the direction of the Rose-Line in Saint Sulpice. It refers to the power of fertility, menstruation, and the matriarchal lineage of Isis. The Red Serpent also could represent the awakening of Kundalini.

The following quote comes from the Egyptian Book of the Dead. "The blood of Isis, the virtue of Isis, the magic power of Isis, the magic power of the Eye, are protecting this Great One; they prevent any wrong being done to him."

The above statement was used on clay amulets for protection.

We should understand that in ancient civilizations the royalty was looked at as an embodiment of the Divine here on Earth. This tradition was alive in ancient Rome, Greece, Egypt, China and Japan. This may be why the Merovingian Kings claimed to be descendants of Christ, Son of God. But in Truth what makes one Royal, being connected to the Higher Self, the Godhead not one's bloodline. The very ancient Kings and Queens from Egypt could claim this, but when that connection was clouded by human ego, the kingdoms fell into power struggles and greed. Everyone has the God-given birthright to be Royal but one must make the effort to realize the connection to the Divine. When world leaders clearly realize their connection and clear their view of separation of people, different religions and cultures - then we will see change in this world as we know it.

One of the myths of the Goddess Isis is how she tricked the Sun God Ra. Ra was not only a god but also was the symbol of the Higher Self in ancient Egypt. Isis had the task of putting back the pieces of her dead husband Osiris and bringing him back to life. She would need the secret name of Ra to do such magic. She enchanted a snake to bite Ra. Isis knew the antidote for snake bites and Ra would need her assistance to heal him. When Ra came to Isis for help, she asked for payment for the healing. And that payment was his secret name. The power of Ra's name gave Isis the power of life eternal. She used that power to bring Osiris to life once again.

Osiris had many titles: the King of Kings, the Good Shepherd, and the Lord of Lords to just mention a few. Is this story beginning to sound familiar? Osiris represented the awareness of the Eternal Self. Isis was the Divine Mother of Matter, the reason she is black. Ra is the very Essence of the Higher Self that is contained within all things and us. Isis being the Queen of the North and South also has a deeper meaning. The Nile was the symbol in Egypt of the Kundalini's Central Channel. There was a Lower Egypt and Upper Egypt, a symbol of the lower and higher chakras and Isis was the queen of both. She had the wisdom of Ra, her Higher Self and she had the magic of inner transformation. The Rose-Line runs from North to South in Saint Sulpice and Isis is the Esoteric Queen of the Red Serpent Rose-Line.

St.Sulpice is associated with both the Goddess Isis and Mary Magdalene. In the stories of Isis and Magdalene, both had the job to resurrect their dead Solar King.

The sundial reminds us of the ancient Goddess festivals that followed the movements of the sun, of death and the resurrection of the vegetation's seasonal changes. The Solar Gods Osiris and Jesus were given the gift of Eternal Life by their priestess queens.

St Sulpice is veiled in a shroud of mystery that points to both secret societies and spiritual adepts that had the understanding of the cult of Isis and associated this cult with Mary Magdalene and Jesus Christ.

Directions Le Place Saint Sulpice, Metro Mabillion, Saint Sulpice.

The Church of Mary Madeleine

The Church of Mary Magdalene did not have such humble beginnings. It was going to be the Temple of Glory to Napoleon's army. This is one of the more prominent buildings in Paris. It is a counter point to Palais Bourbon, better known as the French Parliament. It is not an old structure compared to many of the cathedrals in the city for it was started in the year 1764 and consecrated in 1845. But after many different ideas of what this building was going to be it became the Church of Mary Magdalene.

It is filled with marble and has an amazing marble sculpture over the altar of the Magdalene ascending into heaven and being held up by angels. But if one takes a second look at this sculpture of the Magdalene - she looks pregnant. This of course could be questioned since many artists like to paint a full-bodied woman. But it does raise the question when looking upon this masterpiece. There is a second masterpiece above the altar, the mosaic of Mary Magdalene kneeling before Christ with her alabaster jar (created by Charles Lameire). This mosaic also contains a line up of the saints and the Disciples of Christ.

View from the Magdalene Church

But what might raise an eyebrow or two is when you stand on the stairs in the front of the Church of Mary Magdalene and look directly down the street you will find the Place de la Concorde and in the center of the square and you will see an Egyptian obelisk. The obelisk is known as the phallus of Osiris, fashioned by Goddess Isis. The obelisk is raised in the major axis of Paris that leads to the Louvre Museum, the Arc du Carrousel, the Arc de Triomphe and La Defense. The Church of Mary Madeleine is on the second minor axis of Paris. There is one long street between the obelisk and the Church of Mary Madeleine. This street has the appearance of a shaft in direct alignment with the church. This may be why the statue of Magdalene in the church is looking so pregnant!

This obelisk is over 3000 years old and was carved during the reign of Ramses II. It came from the Temple of Luxor. The ruler Muhammad Ali gave it as a gift to France from the Egyptian government in the year of 1826.

This architectural design of Paris is all relatively new compared to the older parts of the city. But again the connection of Isis and Mary Magdalene seems to exist in the eyes of the city planners. Those who designed the city must have understood these secrets.

There is a beautiful fountain, filled with mythical creatures in Place de la Concorde. The fountain has sculptures of black half naked women and men with dragon/serpent tails, which are all fertility symbols of the Wouivre, (Ley-Lines).

The center of the fountain is made of sculptured boat hulls with the emblem of Paris. Some people think that the emblem may have deeper associations with the Boat of Isis. Black Isis is connected with the Black Virgins of France. Black symbolizes fertility.

The Place de la Concorde has somewhat a bloody history. This was the place where 1119 people, including Maria Antoinette and Louis 16th, were beheaded. The erecting the Luxor Obelisk in Place de la Concorde was a way of healing the memories of the past. Again we see the hand of Goddess Isis touching Paris.

Hymns of Isis
www.sacred-texts.com
"O thou most holy and eternal Saviour of the human race,
and ever most magnificent in thy tender care of mankind,
unto the hazard of our sorrow thou givest the sweet affection"

The Hymn of Osiris
"Hail, thou en-lightener of those who are in the underworld,
that they may see the sunlight."

Directions: Pl de la Madeleine, 75008, Metro Madeleine
From the stairs of the Church de la Madeleine walk directly up the street
to visit Place de la Concorde.

The Church of Saint Etienne du Mont
St. Genevieve

St. Genevieve is the patron saint who took the place of the Goddess Isis as Paris became Christianized. The old Goddesses faded into the Christian saints, leaving traces in their stories, archetypes and legends. Isis held the Ankh of Life and St. Genevieve holds the Keys of Life.

You can find a wonderful and sometimes miraculous shrine to Genevieve in the Church of Saint Etienne. This is one of my favorite shrines to visit when I am in the city. This church sometimes goes unnoticed among the major tourist attractions in Paris, but the history of Saint Genevieve should not be overlooked when visiting this great city.

St. Genevieve lived between 422 until 512. She lived in a small village outside of Paris named Nanterre. St. Germain of Auxerre had stopped in Genevieve's village to preach to multitudes of people. He noticed this young girl in the crowd and encouraged her to devote her life to God. He foretold Genevieve's future and said she would encourage other women also to come into the fold of God's Grace. When Genevieve's parents died she moved to Paris and lived with her Godmother. She began to live a life of austerities. She did not eat meat and fasted from food altogether twice a week. She also lived a life of prayer and meditation.

The Bishop of Paris appointed Genevieve to look after a number of other women that also had taken up a religious life style. In the year of 451 Attila the Hun was getting ready to attack Paris and the inhabitants of the city were in fear of Attila taking Paris. It is said that St. Genevieve and her circle of virgins began to fast and pray. Attila the Hun then surprisingly turned his attention to another conquest in Gaul and Paris was saved from his army's wrath.

Genevieve was also associated with the Merovingian King Clovis the first king of France. The father of Clovis, King Childeric, took over the city of Paris and left the people starving. Saint Genevieve took a boat down the river to neighboring villages, bringing back food, bread and grains for the people of Paris. This particular story of Genevieve may have been overshadowed by the myth of Isis. The festival of Isis comes with the flooding of the Nile during this time they offered Isis the following praises: **"Thou art the bringer of food. Thou fillest the storehouses. Thou heapest the harvest high with corn and granaries, and thou hast care for both the poor and the needy."** Isis filled her magical boat to distribute food to her people.

The plague broke out in Paris in the year of 1129. This plague had killed over 14,000 people. Saint Genevieve sacred relics were in the church. The Parisians decided to have a procession of the bones of Saint Genevieve carrying them through the city streets. The plague was stopped after the procession had taken place and it was claimed as a miracle.

Genevieve's name means " Life Generator." Vie means life in French. Unfortunately, the Parisians forgot the power of Genevieve and during the French Revolution an angry mob took her bones and scattered them in the streets. The church Saint Etienne du Mont still has a few bones of Saint Genevieve that can be found at her shrine. This shrine is connected with the miracles of healing.

I have had profound meditations at the shrine of Saint Genevieve. Take the time to light a candle in the back of the church where the relics of this saint still are displayed. I usually sit quietly in front of the shrine and if you sit long enough in meditation or prayer you really will be able to experience the sacred.

Genevieve's emblem represents the union of Paganism and Christianity. It is the pentacle and the cross.

Her emblem can be found high on the entrance wall of the church of Saint Etienne.

Directions: Pl Ste. Genevieve 75005, Metro Cardinal Lemoine

St Germain I'Auxerrois

The church St Germain I'Auxerrois is a medieval menagerie of sculptures of monkeys, dogs, wolves, rats, bears and the mythical griffons, which can be found in the front of the cathedral. But it is the icon of St Mary the Egyptian that brings me through the doors of this Gothic cathedral. The story of Saint Mary the Egyptian was an oral tradition until it was written down by St. Sophronius of Jerusalem and this can create a whole different story once it has been told several times.

But I would like to share the story of this half naked saint that carried three loaves of bread. Our story takes place around the year of 344 or 421 A.D. The dates are sketchy. Mary lived in the great city of Alexandria, site where the most extensive library in the world was located until it was burned in ancient times. This library was full of many sacred texts and also historical documents. No one truly knows when this might of taken place, but it could have been between the dates 47 B.C. through 400 A.D. There are many legends that have grown around the burning of this library and who was responsible for the burning. But what I have found in my research was that some of the stories of the Christian Saints that lived in Alexandria were filled with veiled secrets in disguise.

Alexandria was the birthplace of Mary the Egyptian. When she was 12 years old she ran away from home giving away her sexual favors to anyone who asked. It was said that she had an inexhaustible appetite for lovemaking. However, after seventeen years of this she changed her ways and went to a pilgrimage to Jerusalem.

Mary the Egyptian tried to enter the Holy Church of Sepulchre and was banned from entering by some invisible force. She then went to an icon of the Virgin Mary. There she was instructed to cross the River Jordan and live a life of penance. Magically, now Mary the Egyptian was able to enter the church after repenting her sins to the Virgin. Then St. Mary takes three loaves of bread and goes to live in the desert. Her hair grows long. She does not wear clothes and the desert sun burns her skin. Fasting emaciates her body. She meets St Zosimas of Palestine and he teaches her the way of Christianity and also gives her holy communion. He leaves her and comes back a year later and finds her dead. But a lion guarded her body and helped bury her. End of story.

I feel what it is important about this story is that Mary the Egyptian is from Alexandria. When the Alexandria library was burned, many ancient texts were lost. The myths of Gods and Goddesses seemed to blend into the stories of Christian saints. The stories could have been a way to hint at the truth for those who understood the secret language of the heretics.

A statue of Mary the Egyptian exists in the Church of St. Germain l'Auxerrois, but there is also a stain glass window of Mary Magdalene. Both of these saints have something in common. Mary the Egyptian was banned from the Church of Sepulchre. The Church of Sepulchre is the place of Christ's tomb where Mary Magdalene brings sweet spice for Christ's body. It is only after Mary the Egyptian goes to the icon of the Virgin Mary, symbolically conforms to the Church policy of celibacy, is she allowed into the church. The Church portrayed them both to have been prostitutes.

Mary Magdalene is at times also repented as a woman with long hair and a naked body. Not far from St Germain l'Auxerrois you can see an amazing statue of Mary Magdalene as the naked repenting saint. She is in the Louvre Museum in Room C, created by an artist by the name of Erhart.

In the book *The White Goddess*, by Robert Graves, the author compares Mary the Egyptian to "Mary Gipsy". Mary Gipsy is known as Marina or Maria Stellis. Maria Stellis is a blue-robed virgin with pearls who is related to the love goddess Aphrodite. When you look at Mary the Egyptian or Mary Magdalene in their naked forms, it looks like a forlorn Aphrodite who has lost all her sexual rights as a woman.

But there is another Goddess under the veil of St. Mary the Egyptian and that is the Lion-headed Goddess Sekhmet from Egypt. Sekhmet was a warrior Goddess of Upper Egypt. It was said that her breath created the desert. She was the daughter of Ra also known as the Eye of Ra.

Sekhmet Statue at Metro Louvre Rivoli

She was the Goddess of Karmic Justice who healed but also destroyed. It was said her body was hot like the midday sun. And her thirst for the blood of her enemies was inexhaustible. It was only when Ra filled the Nile with pomegranate juice and beer that her destructive nature was pacified. The priests of the Sekhmet temples were skilled at surgery,

71

medicine, ritual and magic. Tame lions would guard the temples of Sekhmet.

Then there is the Goddess Durga of India who rides a lion. She is known for her ability to destroy all evil. Most likely the ancient Lion-Headed Goddess Sekhmet influenced the creation of Durga.

We can see the archetype of Sekhmet blend over into the story of St. Mary the Egyptian. When we review the different titles of Isis we are reminded. She is called "Star of the Sea" which is translated as Maria Stellis. "The Lady of Bread" – we see St. Mary of Egypt holding three loaves of bread. One of the titles of Isis is "The Lady of Sekhmet".

When you walk into the back of the church you will find an icon of St Genevieve also holding bread. St. Genevieve's story of feeding the people of Paris is Isis's own story. The Church of St.Germain I'Auxerrois is a place where both the stories of saints and the myths of the Goddess are overlapping all under one roof.

The metro Louvre Rivoli is right in the neighborhood of the church of St Germain I'Auxerrois. There you will find a statue of Sekhmet and Isis with other Egyptian copies of artifacts from the Louvre.

Directions: 2 Pl du Louvre, 75001, Metro Louvre Rivoli

Notre Dame de Paix

Notre Dame de Paix or better known in English, as our Lady of Peace, can be found at the Convent of the Sacred Heart in Paris. This petite Black Virgin only stands 33 centimeters high. She is small, but mighty.

This icon went through many hands before arriving in Paris. She was a gift to the royal family line of Joyeuse, given as a wedding present. Its first place of residence was Chateau de Couiza, very close to Rennes-le-Chateau in the South of France. The statue was passed through the family line and found its home in Toulouse, before finally coming to Paris in 1576. It came into the hands of Charles de Lorraine, the Duc de Guise, who built a beautiful chapel to house this Black Virgin.

This particular icon had more connection with the Merovingian royal family line then any other Black Madonna to date. Part of the reason for this is because so many Black Virgins and relics were destroyed during the French Revolution, so much so that many people hid the sacred objects from the churches to save them from the mobs of rioting people. The Lady of Peace was finally given as a gift to the Sisters of the Sacred Heart in 1806.

We got up early in the morning and took the train into Paris. We came St. Michel, one of the main stations in Paris. This station is where you would stop to see the Gothic masterpiece Notre Dame. Today, however, we were on our way to Picpus Street to view Notre Dame de Paix. This was once the most venerated icon in Paris before the Revolution.

Andreas and I hopped on a metro, got off at our stop and then started heading to the convent. This place was off the beaten path, far away from the tourists. It was a quiet neighborhood. We came to the convent and entered into a very tidy courtyard. The convent was a simple, whitewashed building with a French blue trim and doors to match.

An old stone well was in the center of the courtyard. Sacred places of ancient times were built upon subterranean Ley-Lines. These currents were known as Wouivre.

I feel that Paris is a place of Great Initiation. This old well gave me a clue that this convent was connected to the Wouivre system of Paris. I looked down into the well. It went deep into the earth. It reminded me of a wishing well, a place to magnify your deepest heart's desire.

We walked through the chapel door. A black woman was very busy vacuuming the floor and cleaning the pews. I took note of this symbol. This was the second time I experienced a black women who was care-taking a chapel of the Black Madonna. The other time was when I saw a black nun at the Crypt of Laghet, in southern France.

We walked up to the altar and moved towards the left side of the church and there she was - Notre Dame de Paix. She was raised up high in a black and golden case. She held the Christ child who was just as black as she was. Both wore crowns of gold. She carried a golden olive branch from the tree of peace. The symbol of the olive comes from even an older deity, Athena, the Goddess of Wisdom. A Greek myth tells the story of how the great city of Athens held a contest for the Gods. Whoever brought the city the most perfect gift would bear the city's name. Athena brought the olive tree, the tree of Peace.

Athena was introduced into France by the Romans and was known as the Goddess Minerva. It is interesting to note that the Cathars acknowledged the Goddess of Wisdom. One of their castles was called Castle of Minerva, where 180 people were burned to death in 1210 at the beginning of the Inquisition.

There is also a connection to the Goddess Athena in Toulouse were there had been a Pallas Athena temple, one of the previous homes of this petite icon. Rennes-le-Chateau is located in a region were the Cathars lived before the Albigensian Crusade. This Crusade was formed by the Catholic Church of Rome to wipe out the Gnostic religion of the Cathars. Interesting places this Black Virgin had traveled through before coming to Paris…

Andreas settled down for meditation in the wooden pews behind me, but I needed to stand before this Vierge Noire. I wanted to fully experience her presence. The icon's base showed the words that read La Reine de la Paix - the Queen of Peace.

The woman was still cleaning and the vacuum cleaner was still going strong. Ah, I thought, is this not just the way? When we are spiritually challenged, we are asked to find peace inside ourselves in the middle of the karmic cleaning process of our lives. Her cleaning became a metaphor of the moment. I stood before the Black Madonna. Tears started running down my cheeks spontaneously. My body became electric with Kundalini currents. This serpentine energy moved through me like a coiled cobra rising. I am not new to this type of experiences - they often happen when I am in the Presence of the Sacred. I poured my prayers out from the silent thoughts of my own inner sanctuary. I presented the burdens of my own soul at her feet. People ran through my mind. Relationships that had been less then harmonious - I gave them to this Holy Black Mother before me. Wisdom is won from the lessons that are learned along the spiritual path. That wisdom comes often with a high price tag. But understanding our own lessons in this Great Play of Life, letting go and forgiving - brings Peace.

The woman's vacuum cleaner stopped. It was silent at last. Peace both inside and outside. The release had been complete. A group of people came into the church. Andreas got up and we went along our way.Once we stepped outside, I looked down the stone well. It was a deep well.

Notre Dame de Paix is in the 12th district of Paris at 35 rue Picpus. It is open to the public from 10:00 AM to 12:00 Noon and reopens from 2:00 PM- 4:00 PM

Directions: Nuns of the Sacred Heart, 35 rue de Picpus, Metro Picpus. Open daily.
 Open 9-12, then closed 2-4 and open again 4-6

Notre Dame de Bonne Deliverance in Neuilly-sur-Seine

We took the train into Paris today. We were on the trail of another Black Virgin. This one was on the outskirts of Paris, **Notre-Dame de Bonne Délivrance.**

We walked though an iron gate, then went around the corner and followed the sign to La Chapel. We passed by two old metal flowerpots with the faces of the old gods and goddesses. I noticed the black face of Isis on one of the flowerpots.

We walked a little further until we were in front of the simple chapel. We walked into a vibration that was pure and clean. You could feel real spiritual practice taking place in this space.

Many of the churches we have visited on our journey felt burdened down with people's thoughts, guilt, sin, or just tourists visiting without any spiritual purpose. True meditation is not always present in these places of worship. The ghost of the past haunts the old churches. It is not able to release itself. Therefore, it hides itself between the world of spirit and the world of form.

But this was not the case with this chapel. The church was taken care of both outwardly and inwardly. There she was --- **Notre-Dame**. Her face was as dark as the night. She was draped with the robes of a medieval queen. She held the Christ child - just as dark as she was - in her arm. With her other hand she held the royal Fleur de Lis. This was her scepter of power.

She was one of the most beautiful Black Virgins I have ever seen. She was carved from a piece of solid limestone in the 15th century. Her blue robe also was filled with golden Fleurs de Lis, the symbol of the French kings. The Iris, which is the Fleur de Lis, is the symbol of the womb and the Mother's fertility.

Andreas and I began to settle in the wooden pew's benches that squeaked with every movement. We both went into meditation and the benches followed our silence. I began with my eyes closed but soon opened them: I really needed to look at this Black Madonna's beauty.

This may be difficult for some people to understand. A religious statue - the so-called graven image - actually can be a powerful gateway into the Divine Experience. Centuries of prayers create a living portal through which the Sacred can travel. If you can realize how many people have laid their prayers at the feet of such a statue and that some of those people actually were saints, you begin to understand why prayers can be answered here and miracles can take place within the highly charged atmosphere of the statue.

My eyes became fixed upon the Madonna's Presence. The edges of the statue began to fade and her body and hair turned into radiating golden light.

My visions sharpened in front of my eyes. First her face looked like Aphrodite with hair of gold. Then it faded and I began to see one half of the statue as the body of Christ and the other half as the body of the Black Virgin. It reminded me of a statue I once saw of Shiva, as half man and half woman. I heard her voice inside of me saying, *I AM the marriage of Christ in matter.*

The Black Madonna is the link that erases the separation in Christianity: The separation of spirit and matter, spirit and nature, and the final frontier: spirit and sex. Her dark womb, moist with the rich fertility of the Earth, is made ripe to receive the CHRIST CONSCIOUSNESS. That consciousness that lay like Sleeping Beauty waiting for the right moment to be kissed and be awakened from the dream of human suffering and remember one's DIVINE INHERITANCE.

She is the marriage of Heaven and Earth. I began to pray for everyone I could think of and everyone I loved. Then I turned my heart towards the kingdom of nature. The Sylphs who bring us the very breath of life. The Salamanders who carry the spark of fire within all of creation. The Undines who bring us the blessings of water, rain and snow on top of the mountains. The gnomes who build all the beauty and forms in our natural world. I offered the spirits of nature at her feet.

We returned home on the train and a rainstorm began. We watched lightning streak across a dark-gray Parisian sky. We stepped off the train. We had no umbrellas to keep the rain off our heads. But we ventured out of the station.

As we walked, lightning continued to brighten the sky. I counted the seconds to measure how close the thunderclaps would follow. Un, deux, trois, quatre ...

The rain let up but the lightening still showed across our view. Walking by a wheat field we heard birds singing and rejoicing as lightning touched the Earth on the horizon. The electrical charge in the air was growing and all the inhabitants of the field enjoyed the energy. It was the wedding of Earth and Sky.

Directions: St. Thomas of Villeneuve, 52 Boulevard d'Argenson Metro: Neuilly-sur-Seine.

Note: Make sure you go to the boulevard and not rue. These are two streets by the same name.

Sacred Steps

Lady Guadalupe in Notre Dame

I have been living in Europe for the last two years and it feels Paris is my home away from home. Today I went to Notre Dame to light a candle.

There is a sacred way of walking that I enjoy. I practice it whether I am walking up the trails of Mt. Shasta or slowly through the great cathedrals of Paris. I say a mantra in the silence of my own mind. I find a rhythm for the mantra, my breathing and my steps so that all three work together in unison. This is a simple way to approach the sacred. Sometimes also I like to add a visualization. I see roses of light leaving the soles of my feet upon each step. I do the visualization just to keep my focus. But if I lose both the visualization and the mantra in the process of walking and I find myself just falling into Silence or just being, then I allow this to happen.

When you approach Notre Dame, you enter the arched door on the right side but you always leave the cathedral by the left door. The Sacred Architecture of Notre Dame with its ceiling made of many arches inspires the feeling of traveling though the womb of the Great Mother. When I entered the church I began a silent recitation of the mantra *Kyrie Eleison, Christi Eleison.* This means *God have mercy, Christ have mercy.*

I stopped in front of the Great Rose Windows, which I feel are the very heart of Notre Dame. Then I walk to the statue of Our Lady of Paris, next to the main altar. I purchase a candle and place it among many flickering candles, which represent the many prayers that have been made at the feet of the Virgin.

I stand up and begin to meditate on the Rose Window. I let my eyes take in all the colors of blue, violet, red and green. This seems to me like the first form of color therapy of the ancients. The stain glass window was used as a form of meditation to visually see the divine form.

The sunlight streaming though the colored window provided subtle healing effects. It is unfortunate that so many people walk by these great masterpieces of glass without ever knowing the deep secrets of silently meditating on the color and forms of the Notre Dame Rose Windows. At one time initiates spent hours meditating in front of these beautiful stain glass windows so that their consciousness could open to the Sacred.

I let my eyes travel though the different images of color and light that I found in the Rose Window Mandala. First I would start in the center of the window and travel outwards. Then again from the outside of the Mandala, back into the center. Such is life. I make my journey in the outer world and then return to journey inside, toward the interior of my soul. I paused for a while, enjoying my color meditation and then I returned to my sacred walk though the cathedral, all the while saying the mantra within my mind. I did not hurry. This was my sacred moment to touch the deep parts of myself. I took the time to enjoy the images of the Life of Christ carved in wood and beautifully painted as they are displayed in the back of Notre Dame.

I always stop to say hello to Our Lady Guadalupe, who is Our Lady of both North and South America. One of the titles of Lady Guadalupe is the "Empress of the Americas". Her shrine is well visited here in Notre Dame and she always has many flickering candles before her. I make a small prayer inside of myself. *"May her blue mantle of stars protect and bring healing to the Americas,"* I whispered in my heart of hearts.

The Infinite Light is what we find at the very center of all forms. The expressions of the Infinite Light are ever changing to adapt to the belief systems as they may occur throughout the unfolding of time and shifting of thought in the coming and going of different cultures.

This is the story of Guadalupe: A Mexican peasant, by the name of Juan Diego had a miraculous apparition of our Lady Guadalupe on Dec. 12,1531. Lady Guadalupe appeared to him on a hill where once the temple of the Aztec Goddess Tonantzin was worshipped. Tonantzin was a Mestizo deity worshiped as The Earth Goddess. Tonantzin had many forms; one of her wrathful forms was Cihuacoat the serpent woman. The Divine Mother miraculously appeared on the tilma, the clothing of Juan Diego. This was brought to the local bishop and a cathedral was built over this older sacred site.

I had worked with many Native American people over a course of ten years. During this time, I meet an Indian man from Mexico who told me about the different aspects of the Goddess Tonantzin whose name translates as "She who has a Skirt of Stars". He said she was the Mother of the Americas and her skirt of stars covers all of the Americas.

A little while later I had an insight into what this man had shared with me. The Egyptian Goddess Nut also has a body made of the stars, just like Tonantzin skirt of stars. Both of these aspects of the Divine Mother protected two different continents.

The ancient Egyptians knew and said that every woman was a nutrit, a little goddess. This is a revelation of the Sacred that each one of us holds at the Center of our Heart. The Infinite Light, the Spacious Void exists in every atom and within us. Our ultimate responsibility is that we need to master our own lives, our emotions and our mental process to bring true and lasting change on planet Earth.

The negative projections and fear of the terrifying Serpent Goddess we find in many religions in reality represent our own layer of negative emotions and conditioning that need to be examined and purified within our own being.

Lady Guadalupe is considered as a Black Madonna since her skin is brown. It is interesting to note that the miraculous image of Guadalupe is turning black from the environment's pollution of Mexico City. The pollution we find on this Earth at this time in history is the scar on the face of the Black Madonna.

I continue my sacred steps, observing the unfolding and integration of my insights as I pass through the cathedral. I left through the great door and went back out into the world, enriched by giving myself time for a Sacred Moment.

This type of Sacred Walking is an ancient practice that many holy people around the world have used throughout the centuries. The yogis of India repeated mantras while they traveled the trails of the Himalayas. Christians carried an icon of the virgin up steep alpine pilgrimage trails, saying Hail Mary. Their feet touched the mountain Ley-Lines that awakened the land and also filled the people with magnetic energies that had the power to answer prayers and heal the body. Buddhist monks and holy women repeated the mantra of Kannon-sama as they traveled to the temples of Kannon in Kyoto. Many cultures combined both prayer and walking as a way to slow down, become calm and touch the Sacred within. The repetition of the Divine Names can begin to erase the negative conditions and programs we all hold and can bring us to inner silence and clear perception.

A Standing Stone in Ollainville

La Vierge Noir (Black Virgin) in not only found in the churches but also in natural environments. Human hands do not make her, but her body can be etched by the elements themselves. Certain stones that often were worshiped by the ancients are expressions of this.

We had been staying on the outskirts of Paris in a village called Ollainville. We enjoyed taking daily walks. During one of those walks, passing by golden wheat fields, we came to a lake. This lake was also an animal sanctuary. A friend had explained to me beforehand that there is an ancient Celtic standing stone across the lake in the park.

We took a small pathway to this ancient rock. We came to an open wildflower field and there was the standing stone. The wisdom of this stone had been forgotten. Now kids used it for campfires and marshmallow roasting. One side of the stone was completely blackened by the years of campfires. The other side of the stone closer to the trees was still in its natural state.

I began to explore the stone, looking closely at the lichen that was growing upon its surface. I have found that the plants will form images that can give you a hint of the rock's history. Man may forget his origin but nature has a way of recording what has happened in any given place.

My friend Olivier, who I was visiting, had explained to me he had felt nothing unusual from this Celtic Standing Stone. The stone is asleep, I told him.

For a long time nobody had chanted a sacred song or made offerings to this forgotten holy place of Nature. The spirit of such a place withdraws deep into the earth. It does so for its own defense since so many unconscious people misuse the area with inappropriate behavior, such as drinking, littering or disrespect towards the environment. This was the experience of the standing stone before me. Its spirit had been forgotten.

The Australian Aboriginals have a saying about the land that was used by the songwriter Bruce Chatwin. It says, "an unsung land is dead land since the songs are forgotten. The land itself then dies."

I found a bottle that was left by the wayside from litterbugs of the past. I walked to the lake and filled the bottle with water and walked back to the rock. I started to sing a little chant to the rock as I poured water over this ancient stone. I used the little chant as a way to connect with Mother Nature.

The water washed over the stone as I sang this simple hymn. I found an impression of a big yoni on one side of the standing stone. I offered some dried lavender flowers from my pocket and sprinkled it over the rock yoni. This was a sign that the Celtic rock was used as an ancient fertility stone. The stone was blackened by campfires but preserved with memories of days gone by. It was the Black Madonna herself. The ancient Goddess forms hidden within the land originally inspired the icon art of the Black Virgins of the church.

I walked along the forest path, chanting and picking flowers as to fashion a small offering of summer's wildflowers. I found a large leaf of Burdock and flowers of Self Heal, Queen Ann's lace, and Sweet Peas. I took small slender grasses and tied them around my flora bouquet.

I walked over to the standing stone. I placed my flower offering, filled with my prayers, onto the vulva-shaped mound. When I placed it there, all at once the frogs from the lake began to croak. The wind awakened in the trees and moved in my direction. My offering had been accepted. We returned to this stone recently and discovered a fence now protected it.

Directions: Take the RER C (Deba Train) from St. Michel station to Egli. Now see http://maps.google.com/maps?hl=en&q=ollainville%20france&um=1&ie=UTF-8&sa=N&tab=wl

The Labyrinth of Chartres

I planned my trip to Chartres weeks ahead of time. I made sure that we went on Friday, the only day the labyrinth was open for the public to walk. I had walked a Labyrinth before but never the great Labyrinth of Chartres. We arrived in Chartres, which is about 50 miles outside of Paris or 80 kilometers.

The medieval cathedral of Chartres is considered one of greatest Gothic designs known to man. This area was once the sacred oak grove of the Carnutes, an ancient Celtic tribe of the Iron Age. This was a sacred place for the Carnutes to visit. Once a year they would gather for ceremony and tribal business.

They worshipped the Goddess in the form of Virgo Paritura in a grotto next to a sacred well. This aspect of the Goddess was a Virgin giving birth to a child. The Catholic Church went as far as claiming that the Virgin Mary was worshipped at Chartres before the birth of Christ. The Carnute's grotto had a rock that was in the shape of the Mother Goddess vulva. The Crypt was built over the grotto. The sacred well is now called The Well of Saint Forts. Notre Dame Sous Terre, Our Lady of the Underground is now the Virgin of the Chartres Crypt. The original statue was burned in front of Chartres during the French Revolution in December of 1793. It was later replaced with a 19th century statue when the Crypt was restored in 1976. This statue is said to be close to the original that was burnt. During the 13th century Chartres was a great pilgrimage. It could be compared to what Lourdes is today. The crypt at that time was used like a hospital for the sick pilgrims.

Chartres has also been called "Visible Soul". Even though Chartres had been burned six different times and rebuilt in its history, it is still the home of some of the medieval rare treasures.

The icon sculptures that are part of the structure of the outside of cathedral were built by Master Masons. But there is no record of who were the architects of Chartres or the artists that crafted the cathedral. But we do know that the Gothic Style of cathedral building came into existence around 1130. St Bernard of Clairvaux was the inspiration of the Knights Templar who were the Master Masons of the time. St. Bernard was devoted to the Black Virgin and he was also known to have visions of Our Lady. His experiences could have been the inspiration of creating cathedral buildings dedicated to the Virgin Mary. Many of the Knights Templar Masons were influenced during the Crusades to the Holy Land. Islamic Art, Science and Astrology had inspired the Templars, and this was one of the influences of the cathedral building at the time.

The front door of Chartres is known as the Royal Portal because this was the way the Kings and Queens would enter the church. The sculptures there portray the Ascension of Christ into Heaven, the assembly of the Apostles, Saints and images of royalty. Each door of Chartres is surrounded by images and symbolism. One could spend days just studying these images. I would suggest buying a "Chartres Guide of Cathedral" in the gift store of the church. This would be a good investment to understand the different images that Chartres offers.

Chartres stain glass windows are considered some the most beautiful windows of their time period. They were known as Alchemical Glass, since the secrets of creating the blue hues of this stain glass were unknown. This particular blue color is called Violet-le-duc or Chartres Blue. But now we know that the artists used a sodium compound in their glass making. The stain glass windows of Chartres tells the stories of the childhood of Christ, the Last Judgment, the lives of saints and heroes. The Zodiac window shows the twelve astrological signs but also the way of life of the people during the medieval time period.

It is interesting to note that the Rose Window and the Labyrinth are both 40 feet in diameter. The Rose Window symbolizes the womb of the Virgin Mary, while the Labyrinth is the womb of the Black Virgin, or Earth Goddess.

There is also a stain glass window of Saint Anne. This window represents the oldest Black Madonna of Chartres. The window of Saint Anne was a gift from Saint Louie, King of France, given in the 12th century. The ancient worship of the crone aspect of the pagan Goddess resurfaced in Christianity and became the cult of Saint Anne during this time period.

Notre Dame du Pilier, Our Lady of the Pillar, is another Black Virgin found in the nave of the cathedral. She is made of pear wood and is dressed in royal robes of white and gold. She stands on a pillar holding the Christ Child. This beautiful icon is well worth sitting with in meditations to experience the power that the Black Virgins can contain. She was donated to Chartres after the French Revolution so she would not be considered one of the older icons of the church, but her presence does command respect.

One of the most sacred relics in the Cathedral of Chartres is the Sancta Camisia, the holy tunic of Mary. She wore this tunic while birthing the Christ child. The tunic was donated to the cathedral in the year of 876 and was brought back from the crusades in the Holy Land. This Holy Relic had been used to bless the queens of France to ease their labors of childbirth. During one of the fires of Chartres the tunic was believed to be lost in the flames, but was miraculously saved and found three days later. This was seen as a miracle to the town's people and the reconstruction plans for the cathedral began with a new hope and vigor.

One of the most important reasons for me to come to Chartres was to walk the Labyrinth. The Labyrinth of Chartres has eleven circuits and was built around 1200. There were also other Labyrinths in Gothic cathedrals in Reims and Amiens but these Labyrinths were destroyed because they were no longer understood. The Labyrinth of Chartres is made of white stone and black marble. There was once a copper plaque at its center but it was removed and melted down during the French Revolution.

The Gothic Labyrinth was once called "Chemin de Jerusalem", the Road to Jerusalem and was used as substitute as a pilgrimage to Jerusalem.

Labyrinths were found in the Cretan palace of Minos, connected to the Minotaur the "Bull of Minos." Labyrinth designs were found in caves, on coins and tombs, symbolizing death and rebirth.

The serpentine path of the Labyrinth spirals into its own center. The mystical initiations of the Labyrinth point to the deeper meanings of life. All our different experiences can be used to take us to the center of our soul. This is the purpose of all true pilgrimages.

When I arrived at the Labyrinth in the Cathedral, I stood outside watching all the different types of people who were walking in it. It was like seeing a slice of humanity before my eyes.

Some people were snapping pictures with their cameras, unaware of the people walking in silence before them. They approached the sacred without awareness or respect. There were people were making their best efforts to have their experience. Some walked slow and others hurried through the experience moving on to the next site in their guidebook.

The question that arose in me was how to approach the Labyrinth? Or perhaps the greater question was how to approach life? I decided to enter the labyrinth with the name of Christ in my mind. This could keep me focused with every step I walked.

When I entered the Labyrinth I realized that I had to interact with others who also were walking the Labyrinth. How walk between the people? It became the dance of life, the dance of humanity as we were all on this path together. I kept my inner focus on my mantra but my outer focus was to walk slowly and move though the crowd with awareness and also kindness.

I began to notice that in the center of the maze there were sometimes three or four people at once, taking their time of standing there before making their way back on the same path they had entered.

My inner focus was on the mantra. The mantra became intense with each step as I came closer to the center of the Labyrinth. I arrived at the center and to my amazement I was the only one there. No one was behind me or in front of me. I was alone in the center. My heart expanded and I could feel the power of the magnetic energy that spiraled on the floor, bringing me to the center of my heart, the seat of my soul. The energy raised up though the stones into my feet and through the central channel of my body. My prayers and my spirit also rose. It felt like my spirit was flying. I was in communion with the Divine and I was plugged into the current of the Labyrinth that moved though me like the electric energy in a light socket. Waves of bliss surged through my body and gratitude filled my mind. I was grateful for the breath of life and the opportunity of being alive. I took my moment and I allowed myself to pray for all those I loved and all those I had ever known. The inner door of the experience began to close as soon as the next person stepped into the center. I smiled and walked out the same way I had entered: in joyous celebration.

Directions: http://wikitravel.org/en/Chartres

Traveling to Northern France: Mont St. Michel

Mont St. Michel's granite rock foundations rise high above sea level. This medieval city was built in Normandy, France in the 8th century. The original name for this area was Mount Tombe because it had been an ancient Gaul cemetery.

But this changed after the Bishop Aubert of Avanches had a vision of Michael the Archangel embracing Mount Tombe. The Bishop dedicated the land to Saint Michael. Michael is considered one of God's greatest angels. He is the vanquisher of evil and protector of the faithful. He is the leader of the Heavenly Host of Angels. His name means: *Who is as God.*

The Bishop of Avanches was not the only one who had an idea of building a great cathedral to Saint Michael. Directly across the English Channel, in the city of Cornwall, a Gothic cathedral also had been built honoring Michael. There exists a larger grid of cathedrals in alignment with Mont San Michael of France. The cathedral's alignment starts with Mount Carmel of Israel, that then passes though Delos and Delphi, the oracle sites dedicated to Apollo and his sister Artemis. The line travels onto the Benedictine monastery of Monte Gargano, Italy also dedicated to Saint Michael. It continues to Mount San Michel of France into Saint Michaels of Cornwall's and then on to Skellig, an island off the south of Ireland that is also dedicated to Saint Michael.

Saint Michael is often associated with the slaying of Lucifer, one of God's fallen angels. Lucifer is the light bringer or the lightening serpent that came from heaven to fertilize the Great Mother of Matter. Gnostic Christians believed that Lucifer brought enlightenment to humanity much like the Greek myth of Prometheus steeling fire from Zeus. But in the story of Adam and Eve Lucifer becomes the evil serpent of the tree of knowledge that offers the apple to Eve. These stories are still about the battle of separation of God from Mother Matter.

It is the myth of duality. How can God be separate from his/her creation except though our perception of duality? Lucifer is the light that has slowed down to such a low vibration that the light has become matter. The trouble with being in matter is that it forgets who it is. It believes itself to be only form. Thus by eating the apple from the tree of knowledge, the serpent becomes the Kundalini rising back up the heavenly staircase to begin to awaken to who one truly is.

Michael is also associated with killing the dragon, which is another symbol of fertility of the land. The ancient East had a better view of the dragons. The dragons are the Ley-Lines, which distribute the fertility of the land. In Asia they built their homes and temples in harmony with nature and the Ley-Lines. The Western mind had the attitude of needing to conquer nature, and after a few centuries passing, I hope we can begin to see that this does not really work.

The serpentine energy of Mont San Michel is very visible. You can see how the tides moved through the sand that surrounds the Mount leaving the impression of wiggling serpents behind in the sand. The granite mound that the medieval city is built on is a dragon line that curls around the city, becoming the foundation for the abbey.

Conquering the land was not as easy as it may have seemed for the medieval builders. The Romanesque building of the abbey went into major construction in the year of 1023. The abbey grew larger over the centuries. Finally, the abbey's foundations became larger than the summit that supported the building. This created the problem of the buildings collapsing. They also experienced several fires in the process.

Then later in history, the French Revolution took over the cathedral, leaving the monks fleeing for their lives. Two years after the Revolution the abbey was turned into a prison until 1863. During this time walls were torn down and some of the beauty of the original structure of the cathedral was lost.

The medieval builders may have thought that they had the help of Saint Michael had who had conquered and killed the dragon of the land. But when I visited San Mont Michael I walked the pathway of this medieval city and I found that the power of the green dragon still lives here. The dragons present were in the stone of the earth and could be seen if you looked closely. Their scales became mossy rocks that spiraled around the village's walls.

When I arrived in the cathedral in the crypt of the Black Madonna known as Notre Dame du Mont-Tombe, I found in the next room before entering the crypt a yoni-shaped rock set back against the wall. I thought this must have been a fertility stone used by medieval women. I touched the stone and made a prayer for the Earth. Then I saw the face of the dragon in the stone that was used in the wall.

I walked exploring the different pathways around the abbey. When I finally arrived at the top of the castle walls I could look out and see wet sands surrounding the Mont San Michael. The sand mixed with water creating serpentine shapes that shimmered silvery in the afternoon's sunlight. However, there were local signs along the roads that said, beware of walking out in this sand! The ever-present quicksand just might swallow you up. I guess the serpents and dragons still rule this land. Saint Michael did not kill them. They were just tamed a little.

Mont San Michel once had a Black Virgin that had been brought back from the Holy Land in 867 but was lost during the historical changes. The original Black Virgin was replaced by the monks in 1966 and now can be found in the Crypt.

There is a very powerful golden statue of Saint Michael in the upper floor of the Abbey, which is very impressive. There are also traditional cloistered gardens typical for the medieval time period.

I was amazed to see a giant wooden wheel that opened the castle door. I realized that this was the inspiration used for the Wheel of Fortune card that is found in older tarot decks. The Wheel of Fortune card is symbolic of karmic change.

Mont San Michael is a major tourist site and you should be ready for crowds of people, but it is worth the visit just to see the view from the top of the castle's walls.

Directions:
http://goeurope.about.com/od/montsaintmichel/l/bl_mont_st_michel_map.htm

Central France: The Black Madonna of Lyon

Our friend Solange invited us to the city of Lyon as guests. The famous Basilica of Lyon has a shrine to La Vierge Noire. It is fascinating to note that this great cathedral had been built over an ancient temple to the Goddess Aphrodite.

Two of the great rivers of France were at the very heart of the city: the river Rhone and Saone. They flowed together side by side. The ancients believed when two rivers meet, this is a place of power.

Lyon's older name was Lugdunum. During the ancient times it was the capital of Gaul. It was named after the Celtic God Lug. Lug was the honored God of the first grains that were harvested. His celebration was on August 1, at Lammas (loaf mass). Later the city became a part of the Roman Empire. Lyon became an intersection where the great roads of Rome met. Here the Romans built aqueducts, public baths, forums and theaters. Lyon was the ancient city dedicated to the Goddess Cybele.

The Mother Goddess Cybele can be traced back to Neolithic, matriarchal cultures. She was worshipped as a black stone. The Romans called her Magna Mater. This connects her with the Wouivre Currents. Stones often marked the Wouivre Current's distribution of the fertility energy for the health of animals, plants and man. These stones were called Menhirs. The hot magma deep in the earth and how it shaped the landscape as rock ridges - that is also part of these Wouivre Currents. These are the same type of rock ridges that I have pointed out as dragons in the land.

The roots of the word Cybele is linked with the words crypt, cave, dome and head. The cubic Black Stone in Mecca may have its origin with this Neolithic Goddess. Her animal familiar was the great lion, which is one of the symbols used to this day in Lyon. The Romans introduced Cybele into Gaul. She blended with the Gaul's own divinities that oversaw victory, fertility and water.

In the evening we partook of a light evening meal with Solange and family. Then we retired for the night. The next morning Andreas, Olivier and I made our way through Lyon's metro system to arrive before the city's greatest basilica. I stood outside in the pouring rain. The beauty of this basilica struck me deeply. Integrated into the cathedral's architecture was one statue after another. It was intensely beautiful. My eyes rested transfixed upon these angelic presences that seemed more like Ancient Priestesses, transformed into an acceptable form for Christianity.

The Fourvière Basilica was built in 1896. The Virgin Mary was chosen in 1643 as the patron saint of Lyon. The ancient Goddess Cybele now was being replaced by Mary, who held the position of incorporating many of the ancient Goddesses under her veil. The building of the Basilica was a way of honoring Mary the Virgin as the Patron Saint of Lyon. The Fourvière Basilica has been given the nickname The Upside-Down Elephant, since the four towers of the cathedral look like the legs of an elephant.

We walked down into the Crypt that would be considered the womb and often the tomb of the Church. But the beauty of this Crypt was nothing like I had seen before. Many aspects of the Virgin Mary were lined up along one side of the crypt. I paid my respects to Our Lady of Fatima, Our Lady of India, and The Black Madonna of Poland. I walked by the different expressions of Mary, feeling the devotion to each aspect that had touched my life one time or another.

But as I walked closer to the main altar, the beauty of the womb-shaped mosaic shrine that unfolded before me was breathtaking! The center of this mosaic masterpiece was a white dove, trimmed in gold. The walls of the inner shrine were completely covered in tiny tiles of blue and many heavenly hues that were so pleasant to look upon.

Then, all of a sudden, I realized this was the womb of Aphrodite. We were on the ground floor of the Basilica. The cathedral was built over the foundations of the Temple of the Love Goddess. No wonder this crypt reflected such beauty and creativity. The white dove that was the symbol of the Holy Spirit in the Christian Trinity before was the symbol of Venus or Aphrodite. The legend of Lyon says that the Roman forum crumbled in 840 and the church of the Virgin was built over the Temple of Venus.

I walked up the stairs and out of the crypt. I entered through the door that was on the right side of the main entrance of the Basilica. There, above the altar was the Virgin of Fourvière in all her beautiful blackness. No one really knows how old this statue is. From a passing tour guide we heard that the virgin was once white and with age she turned black. I do not believe this to be true. It is an excuse of the church to cover up their embarrassment over the high number of black Madonnas, which originally were Pagan deities.

The room was silent with many people fervently praying to the Black Virgin before me. It felt I was in a place where people were truly suffering under the yoke of life. They had come to find relief at the feet of this Virgin.

I then went into the main altar room of the cathedral. There was a wall-to-wall mosaic, depicting historical events that took place in France. The mastery of the mosaic was so beautiful that it actually brought tears to my eyes to be before such beauty made by human hands.

My father used to create mosaic murals for a living when I was a child. This art form was close to my heart. The mural that caught my eye was one of Joan of Arc. She also was a worshipper of the Black Madonna. She prayed daily at her shrine before going into battle. The mural showed Joan receiving visions of Mary as a young girl. There was an image of her on horseback in front of Notre Dame in Paris with her army. The last image was that of her death.

Joan of Arc led the armies of France into battle. She was a warrior maiden whose reward in the end was to be turned over to England and burnt at the stake. This was the fate of so many women during that time, to be burnt by the church. Joan of Arc later was resurrected as a saint.

The Fourvière Basilica for me is one of the masterpieces of France. It is well worth the effort to visit.

Direction: http://www.sacred-destinations.com/france/lyon-cathedral-st-jean

Traveling to Southern France
The Cult of Mary the Magdalene
Vézelay, Saint Maximin and Sainte Baume

It is very difficult to separate the story of Mary Magdalene from historical facts, myth, political intrigue and the projections of what feminists would like the Magdalene to be. Nevertheless the Cult of Mary Magdalene had a strong hold here in France during the Medieval Ages.

We began our journey down to the South and along the way we stopped in Vézelay in Burgundy. This Church was the starting point of many Medieval pilgrimages to Santiago de Compostela. It is the home of one the sites that hold the relics of Mary Magdalene. We walked through this medieval cathedral but it was in crypt of the Church I felt the Sacred. The crypt has two shrines, one dedicated to Mary Magdalene and one to dedicated to Christ.

We sat between these two shrines on wooden benches. I felt that I was sitting in the Bridle Chamber of the Divine. It found the Sacred Masculine and the Sacred Feminine in the silence of the crypt of Vézelay.

Vézelay was once a sanctuary for both the Gauls and the Romans. They have found in the ancient ruins of Vézelay a temple and baths. A saltwater mineral spring is there and it is called Les Fontaines Salées. This spring has been known for its healing water.

The Gaul Gods Belisande and Taranis were worshiped here alongside other Roman deities. Belisande
was connected with the fertility rites of May Day, the Beltane fires and sacred marriages.

Peter the Venerable described Vézelay to Pope Innocent the II when he read the psalm:
"It is a high mountain, a fertile mountain, in which the lord is pleased to dwell."

It was in the eleventh century that a cult of Mary Magdalene began to develop in Vézelay. The relics of Mary Magdalene were brought to Vézelay from the Church Saint Maximin near the grotto of Sainte Baume. There, according to the local legends, Mary Magdalene lived out the final years of her life

Vézelay, the Church of Saint Maximin and the cave of Sainte Baume were connected to the Medieval Story of the Magdalene. In the legend of Mary Magdalene it is said that she arrived with other attendants. The list is subject to change according to who is telling the story. Legends had Magdalene preach against idolatry and create miracles while she traveled through the South of France.

It is said she went to Sainte Baume to live in a cave. She spent the next 30 years of her life fasting and praying and being fed by the songs of angels. Saint Baume is also connected with a pagan fertility site.

Our journey took us now to the cave of Saint Baume. It is nestled on top of a large gray mountain. This mountain actually was on a ley-line. It rose high above the vineyards below.

It was a beautiful climb through the forest. There was a fresh water spring, where you can fill your bottles. It led along a wooded trail called the Way of the Kings. This was the path the Royalty used as a part of their pilgrimage route.

When we visited this site I noticed the rock shapes outside the entrance of the Magdalene's cave. There was one very large phallic rock joined together with another rock that had the appearance of a vulva. These rock shapes, engaged in Mother's Nature fornication, were a sure indication that ancient pagans used this area as a fertility site.

Even today wine growers still climb up the steep mountain to light candles in Magdalene's grotto to ensure a good grape harvest. Such caves during ancient times were looked upon as the womb of the Mother Goddess. The cave has been made into a chapel to Mary Magdalene. It is said she died here and her bones then were brought to the Church of Saint Maximin in the valley below.

This is where the story becomes a little fuzzy because it seems the bones of the Magdalene went to different places. It is said she was buried at Saint Maximin where the Cassianite order were the guardians of her relics. The relics were then brought to Vézelay when the Saracen invaded.

The relics of Magdalene did not surface until the 11th century. So it does leave one questioning the authenticity of the legend. There was a time in the history of the Catholic Church when relics of dead saints and the selling of indulgences to heaven became a profitable way for the church to make money. Today you can find the skull bones of Mary Magdalene in the Church of Saint Maximin, which is not far from the cave of Baume.

The Gnostic groups of France, which include the Cathars, and the Knights Templar, seem to have connections with both Mary Magdalene and the Black Madonnas. It is common to find a shrine to Magdalene and Black Madonna on the same site. What the Gnostic groups had in common was the fact that they embraced the principle of the Divine Feminine. Mary Magdalene was looked upon as Sophia, the embodiment of the Holy Spirit. The Divine Feminine included both the wisdom of the whore and the virgin.

The root of this Gnostic thought came from the older source of the Goddess Astarte whose symbols were fishes, doves and the star. The Cathars used the same symbols. The Catholic Church still uses the symbol of the fish for Jesus and the dove for the Holy Spirit.

The Goddess Astarte was Aphrodite to the Greeks, Venus Erycina to the Romans and Ashtart to the Phoenicians. The island of Cyprus is named after. The Egyptians knew her as daughter of Ra; her name was Anat. She was the ruler of fertility, sexuality and war. Even King Solomon in all his glory honored her with a temple. She was a manifestation of the fertility of nature. We can see she had many manifestations and widespread devotion in the ancient world.

But when the separation from the Goddess culture began, Astarte, the Whore, became the "abomination" in the Bible. This was the beginning of the Great Separation from Nature. We all are suffering this Great Separation even in the dark corners of our unconscious mind today! We can see in this separation in our society by the way we treat the Earth and our environment. We treat the Earth like is does not matter. This separation has been drilled into us by doctrines that held only half of the truth. "There is only one God" and that one God demands your worship. Yes there is only one God, but here on Earth in the material world of matter, that one God has many manifestations.

This separation has been passed down through the centuries as the Holy

Word and if one did not follow this Holy Word, then death was the price. Holy Wars are still being fought on this planet over outdated religious views of separation from our planet and from each other. One may not even believe in God, or a High Power to be effected by centuries of patriarchal programming. You can see this every day in the way big business operates. They think the Earth is separated from the people who live on the Earth. The insanity of this bad programming needs to stop for the survival of our future generations. This programming effects all of us, whether we believe in God or not, and has had its effect on our political views, our economic views, and the personal choices in our lives without us realizing.

The Cathars and the Knights Templars realized this a very long time ago. This is why the Divine Feminine was honored not only as the Virgin but also as the Whore. Mary Magdalene held that position as the rejected whore. A Virgin has no wisdom. She is a clean slate without experience. But it is through the whore and the trails and tribulation of life that we gain wisdom.

Who Mary Magdalene truly was I do not know nor claim to know. But as Mary Magdalene, the Divine archetype, she was the wise council to Jesus. She stood at the cross and did not fear to face the death of her most beloved one. These types of trials on the path of life are the real test to cultivate not only wisdom but also compassion. These are the great initiations every soul has to pass through on the journey through human dramas. This is why it is good to understand our history so we can learn why we think the way we do. When we take the time to understand our roots then we can begin to change the choices we make in the Here Now.

Directions: To Saint Maximin and La Sainte Baume
http://www.planetware.com/france/saint-maximin-la-sainte-baume-f-az-sama.htm
Vézelay: http://www.tripadvisor.com/Attraction_Review-g187114-d199024-Reviews-St_Madeleine-Vezelay_Burgundy.html

Notre Dame de Marthuret

We were on our way to the South of France from Paris. I was in the back seat of the car, mapping out places where we could stop. I came across Notre Dame de Marthuret. There was a wooden statue of Mary Magdalene that I wanted to see.

We pulled into this quiet village on a Sunday afternoon. After parking the car and a short walk we were in front of the church. We entered. It was a different style of church than the ones of Southern France or Paris. The churches in the center of France were built in a boxy structure, very solid looking and without the fancy lines. But when we entered the church, we were amazed to find how much beauty the inside reflected. Many pillars were decorated with beautiful colors and flowers in layered stones.

We walked to the side altar and there was one of the most sensuous statues of Mary Magdalene I have ever seen, carved from a dark, rich wood. She lay on her side, holding a jar of balm. Her expression was one of intense sensuality. This is something rarely seen in a church, let alone a Catholic church; but we were in France, weren't we.

We sat with her beauty for a while and I then got up to explore the other corner of this cathedral. There was another Madonna. She too was carved from rich, dark wood. She was holding the Christ child and also her Fleur de Lis wand. She looked more like a wish-granting fairy godmother than the Mother of the Church. This statue belonged to a category of icons called Bonne Mere here in France.

I wandered further to see two portraits hung side-by-side on the same wall, one of Mary Magdalene and the other of Jesus. I thought this is an interesting placement for the two portraits. This was a brief stop on our way to the South of France. It was worth taking the time to see what the treasures the church contained.

Directions: Central France, Rion, Puy-de-Dome at 73 Notre Dame Marthuret in the Church of Notre Dame Marthuret

The South Of France
St. Victor's of Marseilles

I would like to add to my stories the events of our visit to Marseilles last year. Andreas, Olivier and I were on the train to Cannes in Southern France. We had a few hours stopover in Marseilles and this allowed us a little time for sightseeing.

This was my first trip to Southern France and I had no guidebooks to know where I was going. Olivier went to the tourist information center and we found a pamphlet about the churches in the area. The main church was the Basilica of Notre-Dame. It was of Roman-Byzantine style. It had been built on another smaller chapel from the 13th century. The work on the bigger basilica was completed in 1899.This church could be seen towering above Marseilles. It was built on the highest point of the city.

But it was not this church that caught my eye as I was reviewing the tourist pamphlet. There was another church that celebrated Candlemas with a ceremony of green candles and the baking of bread. The bread offerings were called Navettes. It went on to explain that every February

2 the church of St. Victor's did a procession from the crypt of the church with green candles along the pilgrimage trail to the Basilica up the hill. The ancient bread making was made in the memory of the saints of the Provence arriving in the land of Gaul. The Navettes were baked in the shape of little boats. This was all that the pamphlet said.

Well, I put two and two together: the green candles at Candle mass were used as an ancient pagan fertility celebration, welcoming the first signs of spring and the greening of plants. The Provence saints that were not mentioned by name were Mary Magdalene, Mary Salome, Mary the mother of James, and Saint Sara the black Egyptian. Mary Magdalene was always an embarrassment to the church and I noticed it is rare to even find a holy card of her when I was visiting the Cathedrals even though they have many other saints.

I made my mind up right then and there: this was where we were going and I pulled Olivier and Andreas along with me. It was the beginning of summer and it was very hot. We found our way as we walked through the streets.

We came to St. Victors where a class was taught to a group of children. They were charging people a few euros to go down into the crypt. So I paid the price and went through the heavy wooden door. The crypt was under reconstruction, but as I walked around a large pillar there was the Black Madonna of Marseilles. We sat there in her silence. This church was built in 416 and was the tomb of different martyrs including St. Maurice. What seemed to draw me was an archway to my right side. I got up from where I was sitting and made my way through the womb-shaped doorway. There I found a powerful stone-relief on the wall before me. It was Mary Magdalene. But it was even more interesting to find that green algae was alive and growing from the floor of the crypt all around her image. The algae took the shape of a green dragon that covered the Magdalene's back and her hair. The greening fertility power of the Earth was alive and had merged with the cool stone through the Magdalene's image.

Green is one of the colors of Isis in her form of the Fertility Goddess, who brings fertility to the River Nile. The little boats of bread, called Navettes, were an even older tradition than the Saints of Provence. They dated back to ancient Egypt where they were used as bread offerings of the Boat of Isis.

I sat down on a large rock that looked older than time, and marveled at what I was experiencing. The earth power was surging beneath me. I needed to look at what I was sitting on. It was a rock shaped like the head of a dragon! He even had teeth and was grinning at me with his stone smile. This was a natural rock, not carved or shaped by the hands of man.

So here I was sitting on the head of the dragon, deep in the womb of the crypt. I was looking at the Magdalene with a green little green dragon dancing up her back. Now that represents what I call Kundalini awakening, Mother Earth style. This place was older then Christianity. This was a pagan site that saw the continuation of its ancient rituals in Christian disguise.

We came out of the crypt and entered the light of day. We started to walk through the winding streets, following a Pilgrimage trail to the main Cathedral to Our Lady. As we got closer to the town's main path it became steeper and very rocky. I started to see dragon shapes in the rocks along the path as we climbed up to the Cathedral. I looked down the hill in the direction of Saint Victor and I realized the Ley-Lines started in the crypt within the Magdalene shrine, and wound through the streets of the city and hit its peak on the highest point of the city, where the basilica was built.

The belfry rose up 60 meters above the church itself and was crowned by a golden statue of Mary. We had walked the dragon Ley-Lines from the womb to the crown chakra. The view from this church was breathtaking! You could see why Marseilles was a favorite port and trading center for sailors. The mountains were on both sides and in the back. The seaport was in front. It was a protected port. I looked deeper into the mountain ridges before me and I realized there were dragon ridges surrounding the city on three sides. They spiraled through the city to the central high point where I was standing. This was Feng Shui at its best.

This was my introduction to the many dragons that are in the Provence. Dragon Energy equals Fertility Energy. Discovering that Southern France is filled with dragon power did not come as a surprise to me.

Here we have the world's best lavender fields, olive groves, citrus, herbs and foods that have a flavor that cannot compare to any other in the world. In France the best perfumed essential oils are grown and made.

Why? Because the Earth has power here and the minerals bring that quality into both food and scents.

The city of ancient Marseilles had incorporated the Ley-Lines into their Sacred Architecture. I looked from at panoramic view with awe.

If you would like to try your hand at making Navettes here is a website with the recipe.

http://www.theworldwidegourmet.com/recipes/navettes-de-saint-victor/

Directions: St. Victor's is located 3 Rue de l'Abbaye Marseille 13007 France

Our Lady of Laghet

The Lady of Laghet is a well-known shrine at the Cote d'Azur for its healings and miracles. But it was the Black Madonna that is enshrined in the crypt that called me to this Sacred Site.

A French woman we had met last year was our guide into this area. We were going to meet her at the steps of the church. As we were waiting, I noticed how the village was surrounded by a spiraling rock formation around the cathedral. I looked closely at the rock ridges and noticed the bodies and faces of dragons hiding in the stone. The cathedral was built at the very center of this magnetic spiraling energy.

We met our friend and her daughter in front of the church. We exchanged the usual kisses on both cheeks and then went into the cathedral. The walls of the church were completely covered with testimonials of miracle cures that took place for people who had prayed to the Lady of Laghet. We walked through three areas with wall-to-wall testimonial of miracle cures. The areas were filled with flickering votive candles, handmade pictures, photographs and needlework projects that proclaimed the miraculous power of the Madonna.

I turned the corner and entered the main altar area. This part of the church expressed 17th century influences in Baroque style, typical of Nice and the Province area. It was filled with green marble, different shades of yellow to gold and the rich colors of the period. A feeling of layered history, deeper than what could be seen by the eye, was present. There on the high altar was the Lady of Laghet, taking her honored place in the church. I closed my eyes and the silence came to me easily.

But even in the silence, the side altars of the church captured my attention. Both altars on each sidewall had two golden pedestals that spiraled on the side of each altar. I realized the serpentine energy of the Ley-Lines was running through these four pillars, sending electrical earth energy up the sidewalls of the church to the church's steeple.

In many famous healing shrines around the world you may be able to find Ley-Lines, spring water sources, and an abundance of earth fertility. I feel the magnetic forces of the Earth's Ley-Lines are very beneficial for extraordinary healing to take place. What you also can find in such a place are the shrines of the Black Madonna, the Great Goddess of Fertility herself. This is why I had come.

We walked down to the crypt, the womb of Mother Church. The door was locked, but a black nun offered to open the door. She held the key in her pocket. She opened the chapel door of the crypt. We viewed the dark hidden treasure of Laghet, La Vierge Noire. In the darkness of the crypt our little group sat down before the Madonna and child, carved into the dark wood. Everyone slipped into his or her own silent meditation experience.

As I sat in my chair, I was slipping into a vision state. I saw green vines come out of the earth, wrapping themselves around my legs. Flowers bloomed at my feet and the Virgin spoke to me, *'Paint me please. Let people know of the flowers that were once dedicated to me.'* Her words took me back to a time when I studied the plants that were dedicated to Mary. There where 600 flowers and plants that were devoted to Mary, between the 12th and 15th century.

Here are a few:
Rose de Notre Dame, known as Anastatica hierochon
Bonne Femme, known as Columbine
Fleurs a la Vierge, also known as Greater Stitchwort
Chevaux de la Virgin, also known as The Virgin's Hair,
still better known as Clematis Vitalba

I sat in the silence and felt the coolness of the crypt. My vision faded and our little group got up and walked out into the open spring air. The wild flowers in the small open spaces around the church called me. Our Lady's flora was everywhere.

Directions to Laghet:

http://maps.google.com/maps?hl=en&q=Notre-Dame%20de%20Laghet&um=1&ie=UTF-8&sa=N&tab=wl

The Magical Village of Vence

When I was in Vence, a small village at the foothills of the French Alps, I spied a dragon-shaped mound curled up on a near-by hill. As I walked and explored the streets of the village, I discovered it had many fresh spring water fountains scattered throughout the town. I visited an old local church that had been turned into an art gallery. I discovered an image of a green dragon growing on the outer wall of that building. Plant algae that had grown from the old foundations of this chapel naturally formed this dragon. The fountains, the dragon hill and the algae dragon were all the clues that help me understand that Vence was built on a network of Wouivres.

I took a walk into a cobble stone plaza and found a Metaphysical Shop. When I walked through the door I found a magical place full of flying fairies, crystals, and a beautiful blond woman behind the counter. The shopkeepers name was Valérie. I began to tell her about the dragon I had seen in the village. She then began chatting away with a small group of women speaking very rapidly in French. She began to tell me that several of the women had experiences of Les Fey, the fairies, in the local area. They called one of the fairies *La Reine Melusine*. This fairy was half woman and half serpent. Sometimes she would also be seen with wings.

My ears perked up as the shopkeeper slowly began to translate the women's experiences. One reason for my interest was that I had my own experiences with beings such as the Fey Melusine but I call them the Naga Beings. The nagas are the rulers of the waterways and are sacred in India, Tibet and Bali. In fact, many other cultures all around the world have legends about nagas

The Story of Melusine is a European legend that came from what they call the Spinning Yarn Tales. These are stories that the old wives would tell when they were spinning and weaving together. The Story of Melusine tells about a noble man, Raymond of Poitou, who was meeting a beautiful woman while he was on a hunt in the forests of France. He became enchanted by her beauty and married her. But she placed one condition before they walked down the altar: that he was to never see her on the day of Saturday. He made his vow and they lived for a while happily. They had a few children also. But as fate happened, one day he made the mistake of going into her chamber on Saturday to see her bathing. There was Queen Melusine in all her glory in the bathtub complete with the long tail of a serpent. This of course was a bit of a surprise to the king. But before he could even come out of his shock, Melusine quickly took flight, never to return again as his wife. But some say they could hear her wailing on some nights mourning the loss of her children as she flew around the castle's turrets.

Melusine sometimes shows up in the cathedrals of Europe in the stone carvings on pillars. She also has been Christianized as Sainte Venice. This saint is found with serpents entwined around her feet. The Catholic Church adopted many of the pagan gods and goddess, giving them the veil of sainthood. This of course made it easier for the pagans to adopt the new religion if they still had their old gods to pray to.

My own spinning yarn now has become to cross cultures and to weave together the fabric of history that has been torn. I would like to try to repair some of the lost threads of dragon Ley-Lines and the subtler Wouivre currents.

The Melusine fairies were keepers of the waterways just as the Naga beings of India. These spirits were often feared, because they could bring floods, diseases from the pollution of water; and they were known to be the rulers of earthquakes.

In olden days in Asia people thought the water pollution was caused by the nagas, bringing sickness such as cancer, leprosy or other diseases. However, it is more likely that human stupidity and lack of sanitation, rather than the spirits of the nagas, caused the pollution of water.

The Buddha had great respect for these beings since they sheltered him when he was meditating. According to legend, Muchalinda, the King of the Nagas, rose up from the earth in the form of a 7-headed cobra. He coiled himself around the Buddha and stretched his hoods out to form an umbrella over the Buddha's head to shelter him from the rains.

It is said in Tibet that the Buddha was taught in the Naga realm before he came into his last human incarnation. It is also said that he left certain Sacred Texts with the Nagas.

Today in some eastern countries offering are given to these beings to protect the villages from snakes, diseases and earthquakes and bring fertility to the land. If you consider the state our water is in on this planet, it might not be a bad idea to be making such offerings.

The stories of flying dragons, serpentine women with wings, represent the Ancient Spirit of the Wouivre rising from the depths of the Earth and spiraling upward. The steeple of the cathedrals and also the castle turrets that were built on these great power spots help channel these Earth Currents towards the heaven. This may be the real reason for Melusine flying around the old castle turrets: she is calling out to her children that have been alienated by the medieval Church and consequently lost their connection with the Mother Goddess Earth. Valérie then advised me to visit a church in the neighboring town of St Paul de Vence. I thanked her for her help and went along my way.

Directions to Vence:
http://riviera.angloinfo.com/maps/38/Vence+Map.html

St. Paul de Vence

St. Paul de Vence is a village that is filled with galleries, fine art stores, medieval narrow cobblestone streets and several beautiful churches in the Baroque style of sacred architecture that is famous at the Côte d'Azur. There are many shops filled with local artists' crafts and plenty of cafes and fine dining.

But my interest took me into the Cathedral of San Paul. The church was fabulous. It had elaborate gold trimmings around many of the altars. Many votive candles were lit, flickering in the dark corners of the Church. An Icon to our Lady of Lourdes was placed in the church where innumerable candles were twinkling, where prayers for healing were being requested.

There was a section in the church where an ancient collection of the sacred artifacts was displayed. But there was one altar in this cathedral that truly caught my eye. It was an altar that was framed by two icons of two half naked women. The lower body parts of these women were none other than the tails of serpents. I had found Naga beings in the church.

The altars also had the ancient fertility symbols: pomegranates, grapes, poppies, and wheat sheaths. Pomegranates represented the womb of the ancient Goddess. Poppies and wheat were symbols of mother/daughter Goddess Persephone and Demeter. Many of the bakeries in France still use the wheat shafts and corn poppies as decorative art in their establishment. These were all symbolic signs of the ancient Great Goddess, but also they were clues that this church was built upon the Ley-Lines.

Saint Paul, the saint to which this church was dedicated to, had an interesting history before he gained sainthood. It was said he was shanghaied by a ship of pirates off the south coast of France and was put into slavery. It was many years before he returned to his native French soil.

He had spent time at the university of Toulouse and also was a tutor of noble children. But he found his destiny in working with the poor and those that had been abandoned. His organization lives on today as the Saint Paul Society. St. Paul is someone you could pray to if you have a soul mission to help people in need, for this is his spiritual domain.

St. Paul de Vence is a beautiful village well worth visiting. I recommend seeing both the churches and the local shops. I found some of the best arts and crafts I have seen in the South of France.

The Village of Eze

Isis Queen of Heaven

The Medieval village of Eze is nestled on a hill overlooking the blue Mediterranean Sea. It once was a fortress for the Phoenicians but later became an outpost for the Romans Empire. The town is built in a spiral around a hill. There are still the remains of a 12th century castle. It has narrow medieval streets, laced with artisan shops and boutiques. But it was the church of Eze that bought me to this strange little village. The small Catholic Church on the hill had religious art and artifacts dedicated to Isis. One of the altars in the church had the name Isis engraved in golden initials.

There on the wall hung both the Christian cross and the Egyptian Ankh. The Ankh is combination of both the male, represented by the cross, and the female represented by the circle. When the circle was taken out of the cross the Divine Feminine was forgotten. The Ankh also represented the breath of life in Egypt. It can be found on the walls of the Temple of Luxor in Egypt where the deities are feeding many small Ankhs, to a pharaoh giving him gift of Life. I was told that a priest of this chapel believed in the connection between Mary the Mother of Jesus and the Goddess Isis. There is a modern painting titled Isis Queen of Heaven on the wall of the church. This little village has a panoramic view of the sea and is worth the time to visit.

Directions: http://travel.yahoo.com/p-map-483395-map_of_eze-i

Saint-Jean-Cap-Ferrat

Saint-Jean-Cap-Ferrat is another small village along the Côte d'Azur. What this small village has to offer is the largest Black Virgin I have ever visited. It towers over an old cemetery, protecting the dearly departed and ushering them into the next world. The Black Virgin is located outside a small chapel that is connected to the graveyard. The Côte d'Azur area was known also for the worship of the Goddess Black Isis who helps ferry the dead to the next world.

Directions: St. Jean-Cap-Ferrat (Alpes-Maritimes)
Madone de St. Hospice or La Vierge Noire, bronze, in a cemetery overlooking the sea.

San Martin in the French Alps

A few friends we knew planned a pilgrimage together over the next few days. We ventured early one morning high into the French Alps. Serpentine roads slowly climbed in altitude, passing through many small, ancient villages hidden between rock cliffs towering above the road below.

I realized this place was rich in the history of the Knights Templar. King Philippe le Bel, with the help of the Pope, condemned the Order of the Templars. Many were killed and the Grand Master Jacques de Molay was burned at the stake in Paris March 18, 1314. But some of the Templars escaped to Italy and Scotland and some came and hid in this area of the French Alps, leaving behind their influence.

We entered the village of San Martin. The air was clean and there were many fountains. This village had been there since the medieval days. A narrow gutter filled with fresh water ran through the middle of the cobble stone street. My friend explained that in medieval days this same gutter was an open sewage system. People wondered why the black plague killed so many people.

The Alps were the backdrop of this village. The mountains were still filled with animals such as timber wolves, deer, mountain goats and sheep. It was beautiful. We walked to the end of the village where the road stopped and the trail went straight into the mountains. There was the church of St. Martin where La Madonna de Fenestre was temporarily housed before she went on her yearly pilgrimage into the high mountain trails with the townspeople engaging in prayer.

It was said that the hands of St. Luke in Jerusalem crafted this Madonna. Mary Magdalene transported it to Marseille. It stayed in Marseille until war broke out and then was transported to a monastery of the Order of the Templars. When the persecution of the Templars started, they fled to Nice. The statue then traveled to San Martin.

Before entering the church we stopped for a moment outside between two trees. These trees felt like natural pillars, acting as a gateway between the open church door and the mountain resting in the background. I looked upon the beginning of the Alps with their jagged rock formations and once again I could closely observe the faces of Great Dragons in the forms of ridges. But I also noticed a large face of a Giant, who was posing as a rock

I began to realize how the legends and fairy tales took form in people's minds as they looked deeply into the spirit of the Earth. I wondered how people lost this simple ability. The magic of looking for the spirit of nature was veiled. But the connection was still present and alive here and could be felt at this beautiful church.

Yet people do not realize those connections. Or if they do, they are afraid of being persecuted for seeing this reality. That was so clear in my eyes. Once again the Ley-Lines were directly connected to the church and miraculous cures had been reported also in this church. We walked through the door and the statue in this church was almost doll-like.

The first recorded pilgrimage here was in 1338. I realized the community praying and carrying the Virgin along the old mountain trails was actually following the Ley-Lines. This procession activated the Ley-Lines through the prayers and the motion of people's feet. I myself had done something very similar as I prayed and walked the trails of Mt. Shasta.

Many sacred sites exist in a dormant state because they are not activated by prayers or offerings any more. These pilgrimages wake up the power of the earth and bring blessings both to those who are on pilgrimage and to the spirit of the earth also. Ancient practices have a place even in this modern world.

The inside of the church was filled with many old statues of Saint Anne, also considered a type of a Black Madonna, representing the crone aspect of woman. A painting of Mary Magdalene and St. John was also on the walls. When I meditate in such a place I feel the presence of the Ley-Lines under my feet. I have the experience that invisible Ley-Lines or underground streams connect the churches in a village.

This village had many different churches that had the Templar Cross painted on the pillars of the church. Each church had their doors open, letting the mountain air freely flow into the chapels. My feet felt this invisible energy and took me from church to church without any hesitation from my mind.

These days the old ways of the small villages are lost, since it is hard for the young to believe in the old rituals of the Catholic Church. Outdated models of religion are disappearing.

My hope is that the separation between Nature and Christ can be mended and a New Way of the Sacred can be realized.

Directions: Go to Madone de Fenestre, 13 kilometers East of St. Martin by D 94

Madonna of the Village of Bargemon

Our little band of Black Madonna pilgrims gathered together to explore her Presence in the mountain areas of the Provence. On that day we traveled to the village of Bargemon to see Notre Dame De Montague. Olivier informs me that "Mont" means mountain and the word "ague" means sharp or high pitch sound. Bargemont is north of the town of Draguignan. In Draguignan there are legends of the Dragons living in the mountains long ago. I am sure they still are there, hiding in the rock ridges.

We drove on many winding roads, the kind that makes you feel car sick if you are sitting in the back seat. We finally arrived at the church in Bargemon to find it locked and under restoration. But in Bargemon, it being a small town, we easily found a woman who held the church keys. She was eating lunch at a close restaurant. She grumbled under her breath that Les Americains eat lunch at irregular times, and why weren't we eating our lunch like any well-respected French person would? I guess she was speaking about me since I was the only Americaine in our little group. When I reflected on what she said, I thought she was right about her statement.

She met us at the church, put the key into the lock and opened the door. The church was badly damaged, but even in its disarray the Black Madonna held her regal position front and center before the altar. She was carved from Sacred Wood from Belgium. This Madonna's specialty was curing the blind and saving drowning children. This statue somehow survived the French Revolution when many of the Black Madonnas were destroyed by angry mobs.

The old woman with the keys began to tell us another story of a statuette that was part of the treasures of this church. The statuette was called Miraculeuse Notre Dame de Montague. A shepherd in Belgium found this very small statue of the Virgin in a tree. When the shepherd touched this statue, his body became paralyzed by the power this Virgin held. He was not able to move until a couple of people came and broke him from the trance.

When the woman was telling me this story, it reminded me of a Samadhi Experience I had a few years ago. I had been doing mantras to the Divine Mother when my body turned to stone as I was lying down. I could not even move a little finger. India has stories of such states that leave the body motionless. Even though I could not move, my interior was completely filled with the Blissful Union with the Divine Mother. These types of states inspired the yogic rest pose called *Shavasana* or better known as *Corpse Pose.* It made me wonder if this shepherd had a similar experience. But in the West there exists pretty much no road map for such a spiritual event to be understood.

This little miniature statue created many miraculous healings when it was brought into the church and there were still many testimonials hanging on the walls of the church, written on marble plaques.

We were not able to see this sacred object since it was only shown once a year on Easter Sunday. But I acquired a post card of this statuette that had the appearance of an ancient goddess holding a child.

The old woman then proceeded to light candles for each one of us who had come in our little group. We thanked her and continued on our way to find a picnic spot in the mountains to eat our irregular meal.

This is a village church that is not always open and is also doing restoration work. But if you do visit this church and it is closed, ask for the caretaker who has the key at the local cafe.

Directions: Go 21 Kilometers North of Draguignan, by D 25

St. Michael and Pan in Menton

We traveled into southern France and our journey took us to the town of Menton. This town is right on the border of France and Italy. Actually you can walk down the street and cross the Italian border.

We stayed in a little apartment that was decorated in 1940s retro style. We were in heaven. The beach was a walk away. The sky was blue and the trees in the garden were filled with bananas, grapefruit, and tangerines, waiting to be plucked.

Menton was partially below a large rock cliff that in reality was a dragon Ley-Line. I took a walk into the village and found the local basilica located on top of a hill. It was dedicated to Michael the Archangel. I walked up the narrow, medieval streets that were lined with buildings that were mostly painted in the color ochre.

I climbed up the steep steps that led to the church doors. As I walked through the door, the first thing I saw was a very old painting of the Black Madonna. It was created in the 17th century as an expression of gratitude for her curing the black plague. There are many old stories that still echoed the miraculous healings of the plague by Black Virgins. I was happy to see the presence of the Black Virgin in this basilica.

In the next nave in this church was the chapel of the Souls in Purgatory. This was one of the main sanctuaries of this church. It had been built over the older church of the 13th century that also was dedicated to Saint Michael. I was gazing at the altar, the columns and ornaments of gilded wood and my eyes rested on the statue of Saint Michael. He held his mighty sword and stood victoriously on the back of the devil.

But who was this devil? Who was it that Michael's Power was squashing? It was the Roman Pagan God of nature, Pan. Pan was not looking so happy in the role he found himself in. He still had his cloven feet and his goat horns poking through his curly hair, but his face was tortured for he had absorbed the evil projections of the founding church fathers. He had become their scapegoat.

Pan once was honored for his position in the natural scheme of creation. He danced on the Ley-Lines, playing his hollow reed flute. His cloven feet awakened the migration trails for the animals. His sensual, orgasmic pleasure aroused the sexual energies both in man and animal. The musky odor of his own sexuality assured the growth and the increased population of both animals and humans.

The thrilling melody of his pipes awakened the life force of the "Lignes Telluric," the Ley-Lines, to distribute fertility throughout the area. Pan would have his sexual way with anyone and everything. His Sacred Presence ensured the survival of all species. Yes, sometimes he got carried away with himself, leaving broken hearts behind. His sexual yearning did not always connect with the wisdom eye of knowledge and discernment. But he represented the natural sex drive in its rawest form, wild and unleashed - but not evil!

The Church Fathers had to do something with Pan's Pagan children who lived with the green ways of the Earth, following the cycles of nature with the rise and fall of the life forces within the land. The celibate priesthood was also forced to control their own sexual needs, so they bound Pan and projected the sins of the world upon him and called him the devil. Man projected upon Pan, rather than looking inside and facing and erasing the true source of evil that lives within human beings. Pan is a nature spirit and only nature Spirits can act as a mirror of man's thoughts and emotions, for this is how the Creator programmed them.

Saint Michael, an Archangel of the highest order, was also misused by the church fathers to associate nature's awesome reproducing power to the work of the devil. The fathers of the church wanted the power over the bodies, minds and souls of the population.

When Michael wasn't stepping on the devil, he was shown killing dragons. The dragon represents the Ley-Lines that held the Sacred Initiations of the land that gave the people the power to heal, to prophesize and look deeper into the mysteries of the soul.

The Church Fathers went as far as stripping the Great Goddess herself off her sexuality, fertility powers and her destructive aspect that brought purification and regeneration to the land through her winter season, the winter being the time the green power retreated deep into the earth. The snake, the dragon, which is symbolic of sexuality, and also the Wouivre system (Ley-Line system) of the land were crushed under the Virgin's feet. The ancient Goddess adapted herself to the Church's regulations and snuck in through the backdoor as the Black Madonna.

The male sexuality was bound through binding Pan. The female sexuality was bound through the Virgin and the power of the land was bound through the killing of the dragon. The original blueprint of nature was darkened by the minds of the Church Fathers who wanted complete control. When you succeed in controlling people's sexuality, you control the population. The God and the Goddess became only a faint memory, whispered in the wind and the wild places of the land.

I walked out of the church and along the coastline there was a great rock ridge before me and I could see the shape of a dragon within the stone. As I focused on the images etched in the stone shaped by the elements, I could see the image of Pan in the weathered rock. Pan still lives in nature for those who have the eyes to see through Mother Nature's veils. I also found a statue of a happier Pan at one of the fountains near the town's center.

Maybe it is high time to change the archetypes that once were manipulated. Let us see Saint Michael being a protector of the environment, holding the shield with a dragon on it. Let us see Michael protecting the life force of the Earth.

Let us see the dark face of the Madonna who is not afraid of her fertility power, the power of birth, death and purification.

Let us give the Nature God Pan the pearl of wisdom to use his sexual nature with discrimination and with wisdom but not with repression. These are the new archetypes we need.

Menton - The Pearl of France

Menton has been given the name *Pearl of France.* The town is a microenvironment. The great stone ridges of Menton create a natural protection from many storms that come to other areas of the Côte d'Azur. The town itself is a Mecca for the French during the summer holidays. It has a grand lemon festival in the month of February when people from all over Europe come to enjoy a display of Mardi Gras dancers, performers, and parade floats that are made of oranges, lemons and grapefruit.

The town population itself represents a mixture of both French and Italians and many of the villagers speak both languages. In Menton you can dine at a fine restaurant but you can also eat an excellent lunch for five euros at one of the local pita stands at the edge of the town center.

During Christmas time it has one of the most magnificent light displays I have ever seen. Rows and rows of twinkling miniature lights decorate the streets for miles. Menton also celebrates the Santon tradition that is famous in the South of France. Santon means little saints. The Christmas craftsmen of the Provence have a rich tradition of the Christmas Crèche. These craftsmen create little colorful clay figurines of the Holy Family. But the Provence carries the Santon creations even further then just displaying Jesus, Mary and Joseph. They include the common people you would find in a village, like a butcher, a baker or an old woman, selling fish.

Many of the people of Menton take part in displaying their Crèche Scenes throughout the town. They have a map, which you can pick up at the tourist office. The map will guide you through the town to visit some of the most creative expressions of the Christmas Crèche. My Christmas in Menton was one of the most memorable ones I had in many years. It displayed the true spirit of Christmas through artistic expression and the joy of traveling through the street like a child, with a treasure map, allowing us to visit each individual Crèche Scene.

There is one very little shop in Menton, which sells the traditional clay Santons. I have seen many Santons sold at the different Christmas fairs throughout France, but this man's work is above the common Santon. His creations include the Holy Family in a walnut shell. I have also seen him use a dried pomegranate. His little Santons include a beekeeper, a distiller of essential oils, and a woman with her distaff. His shop is a short walk down the street from the Cathedral of Saint Michael.

Across the border, Menton is just a walk from the Italian border and it is worth to walk up the beach to experience the prehistoric caves at the foot of the rocky Ley-Lines. You might notice when walking up the sidewalks that the earth is moving in this area. The sidewalks have been strangely heaved upward and the asphalt was split in many places.

As you follow the beach, you will cross the Italian border. You will walk through a hotel parking lot and come to a museum. But above the museum you will notice two red earth caves naturally carved into the land. These caves have a prehistoric history that is part of the cradle of civilization here in the Mediterranean. In their digs here, archaeologists have found ancient figurines of the Great Goddess.

These caves are the womb of the Mother Earth Goddess and also the Womb of the Ley-Line energy of this area. It is well worth the visit. One of the caves has a faint rock painting of a horse but it is best to have one of the museum guides point it out to you. If you want to visit the caves you can pick up a ticket at the museum for 2 euros.

Menton Tourist Office
Address: 8, ave. boyer
Menton, 06506

Directions:
http://www.whatsonwhen.com/sisp/index.htm?fx=event&event_id=46899

Luceram

The medieval village of Luceram is nestled in the Alps of Provence above the Côte d'Azur. My friend Mireille decided one day before Christmas to take me on the tour of the *Circuit des Crèches*. We drove high up the winding roads to the alpine region above the Côte d'Azur.

While we were driving Mireille began to tell me about the *Circuit des Crèches*. During the Christmas season in the village of Luceram the inhabitants of the village create 400 Nativity Scenes that celebrate the birth of Christ.

Crèche in French means manger. The manger is the feeder for the sheep, goats or cows. The Crèche has images of Jesus, Mary, and Joseph. There are the shepherds, animals and the three wise men.

Along the way we drove by the Paillon River. This area is a mountainous region with elevations that range from 1300-5100 feet. There are also three major peaks in the area: Pointe de Faulio, Cime de Peira Cava and Mont Escobet. The village has two mountain streams that flow though the village. They flow down the mountain and join with the Paillon River, which then continues on into the Mediterranean Sea.

Mireille began to tell me about a silver statue of Saint Marguerite that was riding a dragon. This statue was one of the sacred artifacts in the Church of Saint Marguerite. The church was built at the peak of the village. I thought that the high mountain ridges and two mountain streams passing through the village all were sure signs we were driving along the Ley-Lines. The saint and dragon statue also gave me a clue we were following the Ley-Lines of the land.

We arrived at the base of the village and parked the car. We were handed a map of the village that gave the details of each Crèche location. Next to

143

the parking lot there was a *lavoir*. This was the place where village women once washed their clothes and gossiped with their neighbors. But today there was a small Nativity placed in a fish bowl at the bottom of the *lavoir*.

The Romans once occupied the village of Luceram and Roman coins and artifacts have been found in the village cemetery.

The first recorded history of Luceram was in 1057. During the middle Ages it was part of the Salt Road, the trading route. The Count of Provence use to be the land baron of Luceram, but the village gained its independence in 1272.

We walked up the narrow winding streets of the village. I became like a child. For every nook and corner there seemed to be another Nativity Scene created by a local family. I was in awe with the different creative expressions that each Crèche held. There was one Crèche that was placed in the hollow of an ancient stonewall and another hung from a basket of flowers above the street'

There were many cobblestone streets with passages. We passed though a medieval archway as we slowly climbed up into the heart of Luceram. There were so many Crèches and each carried its own unique expression. There was one made from a beehive and another from iron blacksmith tools. I saw Crèches made of wool, olive wood, clay, loaves of bread, wine jugs, even a nativity made from beeswax. It was an amazing experience filled with the true spirit of Christmas.

We finally arrived at the peak of the village where the Church of St. Marguerite was located. The view was worth the climb. You could see the winding streets, the housetops and the surrounding mountain ridges. The air was cool and crisp. It was clean and invigorating to breathe.

St. Marguerite is a Roman Gothic Church with Baroque interior. The Baroque style churches were once popular in the Provence-Alpes-Côte d'Azur area. We entered the church. It was filled with marble and gilded gold that is typical of the Baroque style. The two main saints of the church were St. Marguerite and St. Rosalie. If the truth would be told both of these saints may have not ever excited.

The story of Saint Rosalie comes from Palermo in Italy. The city had been stricken with the Plague and St. Rosalie revealed herself to a sick woman in a vision. Some versions of the legend say it was a hunter or a soap maker. Nevertheless, Rosalie revealed that she had been a noblewoman who left her life of riches to live like a hermit in a cave some time in the 1100s. She told though vision where to find her bones. They found her bones at the mouth of a cave on Mount Pellegrino. The people of Palermo then had a holy procession of Rosalie's bones and it stopped the Plague in 1625.

Saint Rosalie was not known until the appearance of the vision. She is invoked for curing the plague and she most likely came to the Provence in the time the plague was a big problem. Some believe that the true origin of Saint Rosalie was the Roman Goddess Venus Rosalia, whose symbol was the Holy Rose. This could be closer to the truth. Nevertheless, invoking this Goddess or Saint stopped the plague and that is what really matters.

At the side of the church there was a small glass museum where St. Marguerite and the dragon were displayed. There are several legends of Saint Marguerite and her historical existence may also be dubious.

She was a daughter of a pagan priest of Antioch. She renounced her father's faith and went to live in the hills with a woman shepherd who was Christian. The Roman Governor Olybrius wanted to marry her and when she refused he tortured her and threw her in prison. A dragon appeared to her in jail and she killed the dragon by making the sign of the cross.

There are several different legends and titles given to St. Marguerite. She is called Margaret Pelagia Marina. These were also the names of Aphrodite Marina, the Pearl of the Sea. The word *marga* is rooted in Sanskrit, meaning *the way* or *the gate*. The hidden symbol of St. Marguerite riding the dragon represents the rising of the Kundalini energy, which is sexual energy that has been raised and transformed into spiritual awakening.

The Catholic Church created a doctrine of that separated sex and spirituality. The dragon, serpent and sexuality were associated with evil rather than seeing this same creative energy as a power source of awakening.

Saint Marguerite is invoked against sterility. Remember that dragon energies bring fertility to the land and also to women. She was prayed to for safe childbirth, heal nursing mothers who lost their milk and cure kidney disease.

Even though the archetypes were changed because of Church doctrine, the truth still is there if we look deeper beyond the layers of history.

If you want to visit Luceram to see the *Circuit des Crèches* it usually starts around December 6 and runs through mid January.

The Feast of Sainte Marguerite is on July 20th. The Feast of Saint Rosalie is on September 6th. The village celebrates both occasions.
There is a blessing of dogs, which takes place on St. Hubert's feast day on August 15th.
Directions: http://www.frenchriviera-tourism.com/index.php?do=N4fiche&id=FMAPAC0060000006

Biot and Mary Magdalene

One afternoon a friend wanted to show me the sites of the village of Biot which is close to Antibes. Biot is a village that rises above the Côte d'Azur and once was a key fortress and lookout point for the Knights Templar to keep watch of ships that came in from the Mediterranean Sea.

The ancient Romans once occupied this village for five centuries and there are still monuments and inscriptions that can be found in the village today.

But there was a particular church that I wanted to see. One of my friends who was a sculptor told me that I had to go visit the church. He teased me and would not tell me what was there but said you must go and see for yourself. So this was the day I walked into the colorful village of Biot.

As we walked down the Place des Arcades, the cobblestone streets beneath our feet breathed history. This was once the strong hold of the Knights Templar during 1209. But the next century, Philippe le Bel, King of France, and the Pope of Roman decided to destroy the Knight Templars as heretics of the Church. The course of history removed the Templars from Biot and replaced them with the Knights Hospitallers of St. John.

At one point the Black Plague swept through the Provence and also Biot in 1348, taking the lives of many people. Then to make matters worse, Biot was destroyed by a Civil War in 1387 and for one century Biot became a village of thieves and outlaws.

King René of Provence reclaimed Biot in 1470 and introduced 50 families into the area. The next twenty-five years the good king granted the free use of the land, sea fishing and hunting rights. Under such generous conditions the village was quickly rebuilt.

The Place des Arcades was lined with many small pottery shops. From the window of one of the shops we observed a craftsman create hand-blown glass vases.

At the end of this ancient village street we found the church of Biot. I looked above the church door and there was Mary Magdalene. The terra cotta statue was weathered by the elements of time. We walked through the doorway to discover a church that was a small treasure house of the Sacred Arts. The church was rebuilt in the 15th century over a

Romanesque church from the 12th century. Before that it was built over a Roman temple.

The paintings of Louis Brea (1450-1523), who had been a master painter from the Niçois Primitive School, were displayed in that church. There was a painting of the Virgin of Divine Mercy, wearing a green healing cloak that she laid open to those who needed protection from the Plague. Healing angels were portrayed above the Virgin. She held the Christ Child in her arms and was surrounded by saints.

There are other paintings of many of the saints, including a magnificent painting of Mary Magdalene with her alabaster jar. But there were also other saints such as John the Baptist, Peter and Paul, Stephen and Julian.

But it was the altar on the right side of this church that took the prize. There was Mary Magdalene in gilded wood, with her long hair flowing down a gown of gold with a scallop shell behind her head. It was the ancient spirit of Venus shining through Magdalene's saintly attire. The Roman myth claims Venus was born out of the Mediterranean Sea on a scallop shell. Another clue that this was Venus hiding behind the Magdalene was that the statue at the doorway of the church was in a reclining position. The Love Goddesses - not the saints - use this reclining position. I was pleased to see the art the beauty and the hidden secrets of this church.

Biot is filled with fine craftsmen, beautiful pottery, a colorful history and a tourist office that I found very helpful it is well worth visiting if you are in the Corte Azure area.

Directions: Office Municipal de Tourisme de Biot
Maison du Tourisme 46 rue Saint Sebastién, F 06410 Biot
Tel. 33[0] 4 93 65 78 00

Côte d'Azur - the Land of the Moon Goddess

The Côte d'Azur is the southern coast of France, also known as the French Rivera. The climate is mild in winter and hot in summer. It is famous for its beaches, fine food, and relaxed atmosphere. It is a place where artists come to paint. The gourmets come to shop at some of best open area markets of France and the sun worshippers come to improve their tan.

But there is more then what meets the eye of the common tourist if one digs deeper into the history of this international vacation area.

The Côte d'Azur exists in the shadows of the foothills of the French Alps. The area is rich with Ley-Line activity and this creates a natural fertility for olives, citrus, wild herbs and semi tropical plants.

The first time I came to the Côte d'Azur was during the Cannes Film Festival. We arrived three days before the festival began. I had been invited to stay with a friend for a few days. It was a full moon night and the woman we were staying with wanted to show us the moonrise from a vista that overlooked the Mediterranean Sea. We drove up a narrow winding street to come to a Catholic Church that overlooked the city of Cannes.

It was the very beginning of the first warm summer nights and you could see all the lights and activity below for the preparation for the festival. We stood under a giant statue of the Virgin Mary holding the Christ Child as we watched the Moon rise above the sea's horizon. The moon began to shine its mystical light on the sea.

I gazed at the shimmering light that was created by the Moon with my eyelids half closed. My gaze was relaxed and I enjoyed watching the sparkling light of moonlight on water. The play of light began to turn into a vision experience. The iridescent light took the form of a giant goddess dancing in the sea. She had three faces. Her body was half naked and her headdress was elaborate. She had the appearance of an ancient temple priestess that had been lost in time and space.

It was an amazing experience to see the light of the moon take on such a magnificent form. I watched her dance, showing me all the three phases of her face and her lunar cycles. This was my first evening in the Côte d'Azur. It was not until many months later when I returned to this area of Southern France that I learned that this was the land of Diana and Selene, the Roman Moon Goddesses.

The Roman Empire once extended into the land of Gaul. The Romans were an industrious group and began building roads, and temples to their Gods and Goddess

A famous ancient Moon Temple once stood at Cap d'Antibes, honoring the Moon Goddess Diana and Selene. The Emperor Constantine I (272 – 337) converted to Christianity. His mother, now known as St. Helen, also a Christian, set out on her own mission to Cap d'Antibes. She abolished the moon temple and reconstructed the church Notre Dame de Bon Port that was built over the Moon Temple foundations. It still stands today.

The first time I visited Notre Dame du Bon Port I was astounded by the panoramic view of both the sea and the land below. I then realized why I had the Moon Goddess vision in Cannes. The church parking lot was a perfect place to also view the Full Moon rising on the water. Many ancient lunar priestesses must have made offerings and honored the presence of the Full Moon on this Sacred Ground. The parking lot is used as Lovers Lane in the evening hours. An interesting shrine stands at the foot of the church parking lot. This little outdoor shrine honors Our Lady of Good Relationships. The ancient lunar deities also ruled over love magic.

The Church Notre Dame du Bon Port is a curios mixture of prayers, old photographs, needlework, and ex-voto devotional offerings. The ex-voto offerings had been left by the family of those who were lost at sea or those who had been healed. They contained miniature sailing ships, a mermaid from the stern of a ship and an old painting of a Black Madonna.

There is a beautiful golden statue of Notre Dame de Bon Port that is carried down in a ceremonial procession once a year on the first Thursday of July to bless all the boats in the harbor below. This procession has been acted out each year for over 1000 years. Ten sailors that are bare foot carry the statue down into the harbor.

I would recommend visiting Cap d'Antibes on a Full Moon night to watch the moon rise on the water. I have return to this site many times on Full Moons to pour offerings of milk on to the earth to honor the ancient past. I suggest bringing roses to offer at the outdoor shrine if you would like to improve your relationship or attract a good relationship in your life.

The Côte d'Azur still today honors the Moon Goddess Diana. If you travel on Highway forty-seven you can see an abstract sculpture of three silver moon phases.

The city of Nice has an interesting children's park that is built around an open-air temple to the Goddess Diana. The trees here have very unusual shapes. They reminded me of dryads, which are tree nymphs. Some of the trees here actually resembled the ancient, many-breasted Goddess

Diana (Greek: Artemis). Her many breasts symbolized how she nurtured all the animals on Earth.

Diana had a sacred position in Medieval France. She was honored as the Mistress of wild animals and plants. She knew every herb and every little creature in nature. You can still see Diana in many gardens in France. She stands as a white statue, holding her bow, which represents the New Moon. Her dress is a short white toga. Her hair is pulled back off her face and her hand rests upon a deer that stands by her side.

Long ago many woman secretly worshipped this new moon goddess all across Western Europe. The Catholic Church outlawed women to worship the moon goddess. The Goddess Diana ruled over the secrets of childbirth, the power of herbal medicine or even how to find luck in love. She followed the cycles of nature and the moon. Those who worshiped Diana held secret rites and rituals in the forests. The women of the Moon Goddess were forced to go underground to survive the fires of the inquisition of the Christian church leaders.

Cannes: The Church Notre Dame d'Esperance
This church is on a hill overlooking the city of Cannes. You can walk to the Church from the main part of town. It is a perfect place for moon viewing on a full moon night.
http://www.mytravelguide.com/attractions/profile-79166905-France_Cannes_Notre_Dame_dEsperance.html

Notre Dame du Bon Port Cap d'Antibes:
http://www.letsgo.com/581-the_c%C3%B4te_d%E2%80%99azur-travel-guides-antibes-d

The Temple of Diana in Nice
Temple de Diane, Avenue George Sand, Nice France 06100

Notre Dame des Fontaines

Yesterday we journeyed with a few friends into the mountains north of Menton, to the village La Brigue. Our friend Mireille was our tour guide for the day. She wanted to share this very special chapel that was deep in the mountains of France.

We traveled through a mountainous area, which was filled with many Ley-Lines and I saw many images of dragons in the rock ridges that rose high above the road. Traveling with the French for an outing is always interesting. The cars are often small, which is much better for the environment; but they are packed full of people. The roads in the mountains are rather serpentine. So, if you are in the back seat you are always one breath short of feeling carsick. There is always a picnic lunch with the most agreeable food one could imagine and there is always some form of chocolate.

I have experienced many outings like this now. This was another adventure to visit the various churches in the area. This was the ancient land of the peasants and shepherds, where goat and sheep herds once roamed the land.

But what I found interesting about this outing was the chapel of Notre Dame des Fountaines. The story goes that there was once a great drought in the area. The springs had dried up and the rains where far and few between. The people decided to pray and build a chapel in the forest below these great mountains. But this was no regular chapel: every wall in the chapel had been painted with scenes from the lives of Christ and Mary. When the chapel was finished the springs returned to the land and the rains came.

It was cold. There was little sunshine for many weeks in this part of the forest. The frost lay heavy on the walls outside of the chapel. When we

155

entered through the chapel door I was amazed at the beauty of the paintings on the walls of this church. But not all paintings were beautiful: many of the paintings depicted the suffering of Christ and the horrors of losing one's soul. I began to reflect what caused such droughts in this land.

We should remember that nature is a reflecting mirror for human consciousness. The elements are reflecting the thought forms of humanity. The element of water reflects our emotions through the oceans, rivers, and lakes. The element of fire is the creative spark within all things. When nature absorbs too much negativity through man's thoughts or actions on the land, then the element of fire becomes the purifier of the land. The element of earth is the densest of the elemental kingdom and is a reflection of our physical nature. The current state of our environment today is an accumulation of centuries and centuries of thoughts, emotions, and actions of humanity that have gone unchecked. We are all connected.

So what happened to the peasants who experienced those great droughts? Where were their minds and emotions at the time of this great drought in the land? The flow of water is in truth the essence of joy. When the right amount of water flows in the land, the land flourishes. The plants grow properly, flowers bloom and we have a good harvest.

But if we look at history we will find that especially in Northern Italy, which also could include the borders to France, had many years where there were droughts and even famine.

We might ask why? During this time of history there were land barons that owned the land. The peasants were the workers of the land. It was not highly unusual for the nobility to sell the best of the harvest and leave the worst crops for the peasants. Moldy rye and wheat were given to the workers who often would cover the taste of a moldy meal with wild herbs. This of course depended on the generosity of the land baron.

Imagine being a poor peasant, working the land day in and day out and then receiving the worst part of the harvest for your efforts. Imagine the unhappiness these people endured, their thoughts and their feelings of lack. Now these same people worked the land every day. They put their energies into the earth, their thoughts and their feelings. The elements of the earth just reflected back the same images. Drought is a result of a lack of joy and a lack of generosity. If those who had the power during this time had given fair trade to their workers, the peasants would have had joy in their lives. When we work through joy, the result is a good harvest. It is all connected.

Now let us look even more closely at the world we live in today. Are people in high positions generous with those beneath their station in life? When our hearts are open and we are generous, the cycle of the seeds we sow will also be yielding abundance, not just for ourselves but also for those around us. When we think with kindness towards the earth, the elements will become balanced in the process.

It is time now that people on a mass scale begin to open their hearts to generosity and labors of joy. If we could do this it could create a huge difference. We could change this world.

Even if 20% of the people of this earth could awaken and heal their own mental and emotional structures, this world would look different today. What is required is making the commitment to work upon oneself - for the good of the whole.

The images of this little humble chapel in the woods were a feast for the eyes. Even though it was cold in the month of October it seemed it would be a serene and beautiful place to visit in the hot summer months.

This chapel is open April through October

Time open 10:00-12:00 and then again 2:00 –5:00

 Visitor tickets:

1.50 Euro for adults

0.75 Euro for children

Directions
http://maps.google.com/maps?hl=en&q=Our%20Lady%20of%20the%20Fountains%20(La%20Brigue)&um=1&ie=UTF-8&sa=N&tab=wl

The Church of St Francis in Port Grimaud

We were staying with friends in the enchanting village of Port Grimaud. Port Grimaud is referred to as the Little Venice of the Riviera. Francois Spoerry created this architectural wonder in 1966 in the Gulf of St.Tropez. The site was originally the ancient Greek Athenopolis 2000 years ago.

Spoerry's vision was to create a Provence-style housing, built on a canal system with old world charm but with modern day convenience. Everyone has a boat and there are boat docks rather than a car garage for every house. The small condo size houses are painted in ochre or pale coral colors and complete with terra cotta roof tiles.

We enjoyed seeing young boys handling their little motorboats, steering their way through the canal system as we sipped our morning coffee at the local cafe. But there were also boat taxis for the tourists that drop you off at the beach or the village for shopping.

What I found sacred in Port Grimaud was the Church of St Francis. St. Francis is an unusual church since it is shared both by the Catholics and the Protestants. Each Sunday the Catholics serve mass and after that the Protestants have their own services.

We were there for August 15th, the day of the Virgin Mary's Assumption. This is a very big holiday in France and throughout Europe. I woke up in the morning and went out to the dock to sit and enjoy the morning sun.

There were wild fires burning in the mountains in the distance. The locals informed us that over the last few years the south of France had some bad fires that destroyed the natural environment. I reflected on the Spirits of the Elements and many things they had taught me over the years by my close observation of nature.

The Earth absorbs the negative thoughts, feelings and actions of humans. When the Earth becomes overburdened by that negativity, it goes through a purification process much like our body does if we have not been honoring ourselves with proper food, rest and right thinking. When the element of fire sweeps through a forest, it becomes the ultimate purification for the Earth. Everything is destroyed in its path, but as the seasons turn, we will see new life sprouting from the ashes. This was the process that I witnessed as I sat on the dock, looking over the calm sea.

My friend Albine came and quietly sat beside me. I reached into my pocket and pulled out a handful of roses that I had bought at the local market the day before. A beautiful chant came to my lips in French. I placed roses in Albine's hand and we began to chant together....

Ave Maria de la mer
Ave Maria de la terre
Ave Maria du feu
Ave Maria de l'air

Ave Maria of the Sea
Ave Maria of the Earth
Ave Maria of the Fire
Ave Maria of the Air

Every Ave Maria we chanted, we placed a rose in the sea. The sea was like glass and the roses floated gently on its surface with each prayer. The beauty before me was breathtaking and it brought tears to my eyes. The chant honored the Divine Mother's Presence in the sea, the earth, the fire and the air. It was a gift of song, inspired by angels on the sacred day of Assumption.

That afternoon we went to the Church and a large community gathered to celebrate the Virgin's Assumption into heaven. A beautiful golden statue of Stella Maris, the Virgin of the Sea, was carried from the main altar in the church through the crowd of people. The priest and his assistants brought the Virgin to a boat. One of the most beautiful girls of the community also stepped into the little seaworthy craft for the voyage. What we were about to witness was an ancient tradition of blessing every boat in the harbor with the sprinkling of holy water.

The choosing of a young woman to accompany the sacred voyage was from an ancient tradition much older than the Catholic Church. It was the tradition of the Goddess or Sacred Feminine Energy being represented not only by the Virgin, but also by the most beautiful young woman of the village.

Our friends swiftly took us to their boat. The captain of our ship handed me a bouquet of fresh roses. We took position right behind the vessel of the Virgin and began to wind our way through the canal system of Port Grimaud. The priest was flinging holy water with his brass dipper to touch the boats with the blessings of the Virgin of the Sea. I sat in the boat, feeling like a queen in her white sundress and peach-colored roses. The moment was truly magic. We were blessed and so was every ship in the harbor.

Directions: Port Grimaud
http://maps.google.com/maps?hl=en&q=place%20de%20l'eglise,%20
port%20grimaud&um=1&ie=UTF-8&sa=N&tab=wl

Provence
The Chapel of Sainte Roseline in Les Arcs-sur-Argens

One hot summer day in the Provence our friends picked us up from the train station. On our way back to their home they wanted to stop at the Chapel of Roseline. We drove to Les Arcs and came to a beautiful vineyard that grew around an 11th century monastery. A monk called Roubaud, who had come from St. Victoir of Marseille, started the monastery. The crypt of St. Victoir is the home of a Black Virgin and also a powerful stone relief of Mary Magdalene.

The monastery at one time was the abbey of the Benedictines. It then became a convent for nuns. In 1504 it was in the hands of the Franciscans who dedicated this monastery to St. Catherine and St. Roseline. Now the monastery is private property but the chapel of St. Roseline is open to the public.

The chapel was built in Romanesque style and was in a beautiful estate setting. It is an authentic Cistercensian convent from the 12th century and is now owned by the town of Les Arcs. The art of this Chapel has pieces from the 15th and 16th century but there is also a very unique modern mosaic by Marc Chagall.

When we entered the chapel we found the altar paintings in the deep rich colors of the baroque style. The interior architecture created a sacred space that was conducive for silent meditation. I found myself studying the details of the paintings and each statue.

There was Saint Catherine of Alexandria with her wheel of martyrdom. Saint Catherine was a very popular saint for many centuries, often invoked for wisdom. The crusaders who had traveled the east introduced Catherine's story. She was rich, beautiful and intelligent. Emperor Maximillian tried to seduce her but she rebuked his advances. He then throws her in prison. She was condemned to death by tying her to a wheel and beheading her. When she died they said that milk flowed from her breast.

This same story is repeated for many of the female Catholic saints. They seem to always be virgins. A pagan king makes advances to them. They refuse and as a result they are tortured to death but they always go to heaven with their virginity in tact. The Medieval Catholic Church initiated the beginning of the true meaning of the word propaganda.

Saint Catherine's legend also says that while she was in prison she had a vision of Christ and his angels took her body to Mount Sinai. Mount Sinai was known for its monastery that contained many early Christian texts.

Every legend has threads of truth, but you need to dig deep enough into history to find the truth behind the legend. The story of St. Catherine more likely originated from the ancient library of Alexandria. The Library of Alexandria was known to have many ancient texts and historical documents. The library was burned and most of the precious texts were lost. Some sources believe that the Alexandria Library was burned by order of the Catholic bishop of Alexandria, but we do not know what really happened. There has been speculation that some of the sacred texts of Alexandria were saved and turned up in different monasteries of Europe.

There is a tale of a female philosopher of the School of Alexandria by the name of Hypatia. She was tortured and killed by a Christian mob. At the time there was a great struggle between the rising power of the Christian Church and the Mystery School of Alexandria. Saint Catherine may just be the memory of Hypatia of Alexandria.

The legend of Saint Catherine being carried by angels to Sinai also may have a hidden meaning. Some remaining texts of Alexandria most likely were hidden in the Sinai Monastery. The Church laws were so strict if you did not conform, you were burned as a heretic. The Knights Templar of France were well aware of the laws of the Church so the truth was masked and clues were left for those who had eyes to see. The Templars also brought back many secrets, treasures and most likely sacred texts from the crusades. They had to protect those secrets from the Church. Those clues are still in the stories of the saints, the paintings and the architecture of the church.

The icons of Saint Catherine are often found with a wheel. The symbolism of this wheel represents the Goddess Fortuna, the ever-changing Wheel of Fate or better known in the East as Shiva's Karmic Wheel.

The next statue in the chapel was of Saint Roseline. There was not only a statue but also her mummified body was displayed in the chapel. There is a special shrine that contains her un-corrupted eyeballs that are prayed to for the healing of the eyes.
There is also deeper explanation of who Saint Roseline may be. The feast day of Saint Roseline is January 17th. This date also seemed to be an important day for the Merovingian Kings of France. The Merovingian Kings claimed their royal line came from the daughter of Mary Magdalene and Jesus known as Saint Sara. The name of Saint Roseline may be hinting at the possibility that she was part of the bloodline of Mary Magdalene, the Rose, and Jesus Christ, the Sun King.

Dagobert II, the last Merovingian King, lived from 651-679 A.D. His second wife was Giselle de Razes. Her uncle was King of the Visigoths and their home was Rennes-le-Chateau. They had a son shortly after their marriage, named Sigebert. Dagobert went hunting one day with his godson in the Forest of Woëvre. He was leaned up against a tree and his own godson lanced his eye by the orders of Pepin of Heristal, a rival to

Dagobert's throne. This incident ended the reign of the Merovingian Sun Kings.

Now Saint Roseline was a daughter of a famous Catalan alchemist and physician. He was known to have miraculous powers. Roseline also had a brother known as Helios whose name refers to the Sun God. He was thrown in prison during the crusades and Roseline created a miracle that freed him. Roseline's family's castle is in Les Arcs. We have to ask ourselves did Roseline have Merovingian blood in her veins?

When Roseline died her body did not decay, even her eyes held their brightness. Louis XVI, the king of France at the time ordered his doctor to pierce the incorrupt eye of Saint Roseline. One might ask if King Louis was symbolically reenacting the piercing of the true blood of France once again?

The Chapel of Roseline had a wonderful mosaic called the Feast of the Angels. It is about a miracle of Saint Roseline who was so deep in prayer that she forgot her kitchen duties and did not prepare the lunch for the Abbey. Miraculously Angels came and created a beautiful feast for all to enjoy.

The Chapel of Roseline is well worth the stop if you are following the Mysterious Trail of Mary Magdalene.

Directions: Chateau Sainte Roseline
83460 Les Arcs-Sur-Argens
Phone +33 4 94 99 50 30
Fax +33 4 94 47 53 06
\

Wildflower Madonna

We had spent a few weeks in Port Grimaud with our friends Olivier and Albine. One hot afternoon we all piled into the car to see the Black Madonna of Pignans. But along the way we stopped in the small village of Collobrières, hat specialized in Maroon Glace or better known as chestnut ice cream.

While Andreas was busy sampling ice cream, I went over to a stone bridge to make a small offering to the elementals that lived in the stream. The stream and stone bridge were enchanted and it was filled with wildflowers and herbs. I made an offering of roses and lavender, which I always carry in a little bag in my purse just for such purposes. When we finished we walked across the street to a small chapel. The church doors were wide open and you could feel how the summer breeze blew gently through the chapel. I walked into the church and I felt I had walked into the center of a wildflower, rather than an establishment of the Catholic Church. Everything had a fairytale-like quality.

The most delicate wild flowers were etched into the marble altar. The walls of the church had been painted in such a way that the hues and the patterns of the flowers of the field had been expressed with each brush stroke. Even the Mary statue above the altar seemed to have the appearance of a Fairy Queen rather than the Queen of Heaven.

This little Chapel in the town of wild chestnuts seemed to capture the very spirit of the natural world. Even though the Mary of this church had the face of ivory, I felt the presence of the Black Madonna was close. I then went outside and right in front of the church was a tree darkened by age. The tree held an image of the Black Madonna, dancing with wild hair flying. But what was even more amazing was the image of a profile of Christ present right beside her. Nature had its own expression of the Sacred imprinted on a simple tree.

**Look closely to the naked dark goddess dancing at her right is the profile head
of Christ in lighter color bark of the tree**

Directions:

http://www.provencebeyond.com/villages/collobrieres.html

Our Lady of the Angels in Pignans

It was a hot summer day in Provence and our friends wanted to take us to visit the Black Madonna of Pignans. We drove for what seemed a very long time on winding roads. I looked out the window as we passed by cork and oak tree forest. Some of the land was badly burned from forest fires of previous years.

We came to a small mountain and began to spiral up the serpentine road to the top which gave us a view of the valley below. We arrived at the peak and there was a historical marker. It told some of the story of this chapel of Our Lady of the Angels. Mary Magdalene came to France after Christ's death to live and also teach the people of the Provence.

This sacred site was once a strategic point for the Romans and most likely a Roman temple. According to the plaque, a companion of Mary Magdalene, Saint Nymphe was martyred at this site. The saint's name Nymphe has its roots in the word *nymph*, meaning a fairy spirit of the forest.

There also was an ancient megalith standing stone that was on the site that was built under the main altar of the church. The rock literally is part of the altar. The megalith stones were the ancient's way of marking the Ley-Lines for either religious purpose or to spread the magnetic energy across the land.

It was in 517 that Clovis, the first Christian king of France, and the Earl of Gaulle, had a war victory against the Visigoths in the forest of Pignans. Clovis had a church built on this spot, dedicating it to Notre Dame De Consolation.

The rural areas of the Provence were subject to the influences of the Gauls, then the Romans and later Christianity. Pignans is a blend of all three cultures and their influences. It was during the reign of the Merovingian Kings, (AD 500-750) that the Black Virgin Cult was established in France.

There exist mysterious circumstances in the ways the Black Virgin icons were discovered. They were sometimes found when plowing a field or hidden in a hollow tree. At other times the Black Virgins would be found in wild blackberry bushes. The Provence is very dry in the summer months but even in the heat of the hot summer sun the blackberries are abundant. They draw their water supply from underground streams, which are part of the Wouivre system (Ley-Lines).

A shepherd tending his sheep found the Black Virgin of Pignans. The shepherd's dog left the flock and was interested in a bush at the foot of a rock. When the shepherd came to the bush he found a beautiful statue of dark wood. He brought the statue of the Virgin to the village church below. But the next day the virgin would disappear and they would find her again at the face of the rock. They decided this was a sign from heaven. Therefore they rebuilt the chapel at this site. The rock was an ancient megalith fertility stone.

When I walked into this chapel it was nothing like any of the other places I had visited before. A handful of monks were living there and the church was in real need of restoration. There were ex-voto testimonials along the walls of the church, claiming the miracles of the little dark Virgin.

A real stuffed alligator hung from the ceiling and another stuffed lizard hung over the door. You could see a bit of the megalith stone under the lace of the altar.

There were some amazing claims of healing attested to Our Lady of the Angels. There was a plague in 1720 that swept across the Provence but under the protection of the Black Virgin of Pignans the territory was protected.

Then again in 1753 there was a drought and the harvest was jeopardized. The people made their prayers and devotions to the Virgin and then had a procession carrying the Virgin. Yet even before the procession was completed the sky grew dark and there was a massive downpour of rain.

These types of Holy Processions that would carry the Virgin, accompanied by many people walking and praying, are an ancient tradition in many villages of Europe. But if we look deeper at the pilgrimage trails of Europe we would find that the sacred steps of the pilgrims were actually activating the Ley-Lines. Pilgrimage routes many times go up to the mountains. At other times they lead from village to the sea. The ancient pilgrims were focused on prayer and devotion. These prayers actually activated the magnetic energy of the Ley-Lines that brought health to the earth and even health to the pilgrims. This is why I believe Sacred Pilgrimage is important. These ways need to be returned to but with a new awareness and understanding that incorporates the ancient traditions, Christianity, and the awareness of our natural environment.

The Chapel of Pignans was one of the strangest places I have visited in the Provence but it is worth visiting if you have a connection with the Black Madonnas.

83730 Pignans Var France
Telephone 00 33 (0)4 94 59 00 69

Monastère de la Verne

We had time when we were on our way to Pignans to stop and visit Cistercian Abbey. This convent is located in the Maures Mountains, surrounded by chestnut and holm oak forests.

The abbey was founded 1170 but went through its trials and tribulations over the centuries. It was pillaged and at one time had a terrible fire. Then it went through more destruction during the French Revolution. The monks abandoned the monastery after the Revolution, but in the 1920s restoration began again. Today the abbey has become the convent of the Sisters of Bethlehem. The sisters are well known in France for their beautiful pottery.

There is a store in the front of the abbey that sells high quality statues of saints, the virgin, handmade rosaries and different sacred arts.

To visit the inside of the monastery you can buy a ticket for 6 euros.

The abbey is open every day. The store is closed on Sundays.
If you are looking for a sacred keepsake this would be a good place to stop along your journey.

Directions: from Grimaud, on a serpentine road of D14 towards Collobrieres, then D214 to Chartreuse de la Verne.

Monastère de la Verne
83610 Collobrières,
Tel: 04.94.43.48.28

Notre Dame des Tables in Montpellier

A friend who is a professor of the University of Montpellier invited Andreas and I to her home. The University of Montpellier is one of the oldest colleges in the world; it was started in 1220.

We arrived in the city by train. Our friend met us at the station and we took a short walk to her apartment building. She lived in a very old historical building. Jean Moulin, one of the most famous French Resistance fighters used this building as a hideout during the German occupation in the 2nd world war. We followed our friend up a few flights of winding stairs to her apartment door. We were invited in to be wined and dined on French tarts filled with local vegetables and fine cheese bought at the open market.

The next morning she took us into the city streets for a walking tour. I was pleasantly surprised to see how up and coming the city of Montpellier was compared to other towns I had visited in France. It is a university town and this was reflected in the shops and the local fashions. But right along the hip and colorful scene of the youth came also the medieval history of this ancient town and the two created a harmonious and attractive blend.

Montpellier is in the Province of Languedoc. It was once a center for spice trading. The city was first settled in the 10th century and it became one of the major medieval cities of Southern France. But Montpellier was also a well-known as an ancient pilgrimage and salt trading route. It was a great learning center for both law and medicine. The learned people of the medieval time were open to both Jewish and Islamic thought. This city had tolerance for Muslims, Jews and the Cathars. These ancient layers of history still influence Montpellier today. This is one of the reasons why I felt this city to be different than any other place I have visited in France.

Nostradamus, the famous visionary, lived and practiced in Montpellier in 1293. His predictions are still being followed to this day.

We walked through the streets until we came to the Jardin des Planets. This is the oldest botanical garden in France. I enjoyed walking though the garden and reading all my favorite plants. Then my friend wanted to take me to Notre Dame des Tables.

Notre Dame des Tables used to be one of the most famous Black Virgins on ancient pilgrimage route of France. But unfortunately the original Black Virgin was destroyed during the French Revolution. During the Revolution angry mops destroyed many Sacred Icons. The original Black Virgin was brought to the city during the Crusades. It was said that this icon saved the city from both drought and sometimes the plague. But recorded history states that Montpellier's population at one point was devastated by the black plague

We came to the door of Notre Dame des Tables. The church was old and smelled like a mixture of dust and votive candles. This church was in need of restoration. There was a marble replica of Notre Dame des Tables that replaced the Black Virgin. She was installed in 1881 but she was not black any longer. This Virgin icon portrayed the influence of Rome for she had the looks of the Roman Goddess Hera.

Notre Dame des Tables reminded me of my spiritual experiences with the Black Virgin of Pezenas. In my vision I had seen the Virgin of Pezenas had become all the food, fields, vineyards, and plants of the region. The name of Notre Dame des Tables carried the signature of the vision I had at Pezenas.

In Montpellier I met a group of women that told me stories and legends of the Notre Dame des Table. The group of women all believed the ancient virgin was connected to Isis. They told me stories of ancient Roman women who once lived in the near-by area. They were the worshippers of Isis. As the women kept on telling the story, they said that they believed the foundation of the original statue was now in somebody's basement but was not shared with the public.

There is known history about a ruin that was the Temple of Vesta on a hill called Le Verrou. Le Verrou means lightning bolt. The lightning bolt is symbolic for sudden awakening or sometimes referred to as enlightenment. The Goddess Vesta was the hearth keeper of the Sacred Fire. The hearth is blackened by smoke.

The Catholic clergy often said that candle smoke blackened the Black Virgins. This is most likely not true, but the Black Virgin archetype walks through the fires of her earthly experiences and this is why she is black. She is the Phoenix that rises from the ashes. She is the Cinderella who finds her crown. In the year of 1789 the Black Virgin's hand of Montpellier was burned when the church was struck by lightning.

Montpellier is a wonderful city to visit and it is easy to enjoy the best of both the ancient and the modern world side by side.

Address:
Place Notre-Dame
34000 Montpellier
Phone: 04 67 54 33 16

Dragon Finder

I had met a couple on Easter Sunday at the church of Mary Magdalene in Mountain View, California, just before traveling to France. My friends were both living in California but also had a summerhouse in the South of France, near the town of Ganges, close to Montpellier. They invited us to come and stay with them for a few days. Andreas and I went to Montpellier by train where they picked us up at the station.

We drove to their home where the forest, rivers, and ancient rock cliffs joined, creating a natural shrine of beauty. Their summerhouse had terrace gardens in a forest setting. The woman pointed out two rock croppings that overlooked the valley below. We both realized we were looking at the dragons of the Ley-Lines. I pointed out the differences: the female dragon whose smooth back followed the horizon line, while the male dragon's back was sharp and craggy in comparison.

The French gentleman who owned the house loved nature and took me immediately to a stream that ran alongside the property. I found a small rock dragon that was curled up by the side of a pool. He also insisted on showing me the crypt downstairs under the house. The house had been built right up against a massive rock in the side of a hill.

We finished our house tour and settled in with a typical dinner of the Provence, which was Ratatouille. We sat down on the terrace under trees heavily laden with fruit. The peach and apple tree branches leaned down close to the earth from the weight of the harvest. Hazel nuts poked their heads out of stems that appeared more like enchanted fairy caps. They were too numerous to count, even though for many seasons the trees had not been cared for, it did not stop their process of bearing an abundant harvest. This was a sure sign we were in the middle of the Ley-Lines because of the fertility of the land. We finished our dinner with hazel nuts directly from the trees and went to bed.

The next morning I woke up and began to explore my surroundings. A bathroom door was opened downstairs and I peeked inside to find the massive rock that made the bathroom sidewall. But this was not an ordinary rock – I could see the scales of a dragon! I became very excited because I realized this massive stone that made up the foundation of the house was a dragon. I brought my investigation outside to find the rest of the body of the dragon, but more importantly, to find the head and the eye of the dragon to awaken the power of the land.

The back garden beds were overgrown with brambles and weed. The kind gentleman let me use his garden clippers to clear away the weeds. He mentioned that the wild boars use this flowerbed as a trail through the forest. This is another clue of the Ley-Line energies. The animals use the Ley-Lines as their path because of the electromagnetic energies that reside under the earth. But after the clearing of the flowerbeds I realized I was looking at the dragon's shoulder but still didn't know where its head was.

The woman arrived outside to see what I was doing and I showed her the movement of the dragon's body and how it went through her house. We walked out to the stream together and I was standing on a huge rock. This rock made a natural bridge over the streambed. I then realized I was standing on the neck and head of the dragon and his nose was submerged on the other side of the stream's bank. My body began to quiver with Kundalini energy as we realized we were in the very presence of the Mother Earth's Kundalini Dragon Lines.

That evening I swept the dragon's head clean of the leafy debris and made offerings of little rose buds. I found a white quartz stone and placed it in his eye socket. I sang to the land an ancient chant that honors the dragon energies. We all joined together in the kitchen singing and dancing the dragon's song. The land was awakening by the power of our voices together and by the silence of our meditation after the song. That night when we retired to our bedrooms, a lightning storm moved through the valley and the blessings of rain and thunder touched the land. We bathed in the Blessings of the Dragon.

A few days later the gentleman and I found the female dragon downstream from the main dragon that occupied their property. The streambed was very dry, so we walked right through it. We came to an old stone bridge and passed beneath it.

On other side was the body of the female dragon. Her body was the streambed itself and her neck and head made up the side of the bank. I realized if I had come in another season of the year I would have never seen her. We moved through the blackberry brambles and came to a clearing. I could see the two dragon mounds that hovered high up above the valley. The dragons that existed along the stream bank created a perfect grid of fertility in the valley below. The nature of this area was lush and fruitful with wild game, wild chestnuts and hazelnuts. I was in the middle of a Ley-Line.

Saintes-Maries-de-la-Mer

The next day my friend Oshun and I traveled south to Saintes-Maries-de-la-Mer, the sacred site of Saint Sara, the Queen of the Gypsies. It was a two-hour ride to the Church of Les-Saintes-Maries-de-la-Mer.

This ride gave us plenty of time to talk about the history of the Black Madonna and get acquainted with each other. Our conversation moved into the subject matter of Isis and how the Black Madonnas of France reflect the ancient foundations of Goddess Isis.

The ancient civilization of Kush stretched along the River Nile from Aswan to Khartoum. This was the home of the Black Nubian People. The

Queens of Nubia were worshiped as the Goddess Isis just like the Queens of Egypt.

The temples of Isis spread from the Nile River into Greece and Rome. The Isis myth then mingled with the Goddess Cybele and was synthesized with other Roman Goddesses. But the blackness of Isis was preserved even though her original myth may have become whitewashed in the Hellenistic age. We should remember that Isis came from the land of Egypt and the land of Kush and the Nubian people, where their skin was black as the fertile soil of the Nile. This is the original source of the Goddess Isis, and her blackness remains as a distant memory in the Black Madonnas of France today.

Isis temples existed throughout Africa, Europe, Asia, and the British Isles. When Christianity became established in Europe, the Black Madonnas of France absorbed the Cult of Isis.

We drove into the town of Saintes-Maries-de-la-Mer. A symbol of an anchor and cross, coming out of the middle of a heart, was in the center of the town. The image somehow reminded me of a much older symbol, the Egyptian Ankh. Saintes-Maries-de-la-Mer was the ancient city of Ratis, or Ra, the Egyptian Sun God. Isis Pelagia, Cybele and the Triple Goddess of the Gauls had been worshipped there since the forth century B.C.

Saintes-Maries-de-la-Mer is the famous village where Mary Magdalene, Mary Salome, mother of James and John, Mary of Clepos, the aunt of Jesus and Saint Sara, the servant of Magdalene, arrived in a boat without oars. Some legends also placed Martha and Lazarus in the boat that journeyed from Palestine and found its way to the shores of Southern France.

Victor Belot in his writings in *La France des Pèlerinages* makes a reference to saint Sara, the Black Egyptian servant of Magdalene, as

181

having given birth to the Cult of Black Virgins in many sacred sites of France. Sara is most likely the Egyptian archetype of Black Isis.

The walls of the church had a few extraordinary sacred objects. In a case was the head of a Black Isis with a golden crown. Oshun explained that before Isis was in the crypt with Saint Sara but now had been moved.

On the opposite wall was an icon image of Mary Salome and Mary Cleops in a boat. But it was a large marble stone in the shape of a yoni embedded in the wall that caught my eye. This stone has been used as a blessing of fertility for women who wanted to have babies. They would touch the stone and make their prayers. I touched the stone but instead of praying for my fertility, since I am a bit past that part of my life, I prayed for women's sexual healing.

We looked above the door and we entered through the womb-shaped threshold into the crypt. There were hundreds of lit votive candles. Each candle represented someone's prayer. The heat in the crypt was intense. I immediately broke out into karmic sweats. This phenomenon has happened to me in churches before where there have been many prayers said in such a sacred place. This type of sweating actually purifies you, thus I named it "karmic sweats."

There in the corner of the crypt in all her glory was the Gypsy Queen Saint Sara. She was not under glass or barred that one could not touch her. This Black Virgin was totally available to touch. I stood before her and electricity moved through my body like an ancient serpent that awakened my body to the spirit of the place. So many people had laid their prayers at Sara's feet. My experience was deep but short-lived since a line of people was waiting behind me. I stepped aside and placed my hands on a stone altar before me. Oshun then walked up next to me and pointed to a glass case. She whispered, "These are the bones of Sara." There right in front of me were the relics of the saint. She then whispered in my ear again and said, "This used to be the altar of Isis." The beauty about the Black Madonna is that she is available to everyone.

Saint Sara's origin is Egypt. The all-encompassing nature of Goddess Isis brought her to the Mediterranean where her myths and archetypes changed according to the customs of the cultures she was presented to.

Somehow her presence made its way into the Catholic Church to be dressed in the robes of a saint or different aspects of the Virgin Mary. She is acquainted with harlots and is elevated as the Virgin Queen. She is about the fertility and power of the Earth, pregnancy and absorbs our sorrows at the time of death. She welcomes all who come before her with unconditional acceptance. She is like an ocean of silence from some primordial part deep within us. She is beyond the changing layers of ancient history. She is a living and ever-changing archetype to meet the needs of the people in this very moment of time and space. She opens us up to personal revelation and deepens our attention towards life itself.

The Standing Stones of Montardier

I was investigating a dragon rock I had found in my friend's backyard in the South of France. I had become absorbed in the process of taking pictures of Les Fees, the nature spirits on the dragon's head stone. Many people would love to have clairvoyant vision to perceive the realm of the fairies. But if one begins to look very closely at the bark of the trees, the rocks or even the moss that grows in the earth, one begins to see little faces staring back at you. Since the Black Madonna is the Queen of the Angels this also includes the Angels of the Earth, better known as the fairies.

This day I was busy recording with my trusty digital camera. I enjoy the fairy realm. These little sentient beings are such a pure-hearted race. Oshun had company and it was time to set down my camera and meet one of her friends, a beautiful woman by the name of Sylvie.

Sylvie was a very sophisticated French woman who knew the best French wines and was an expert in Medieval Music. We had a chance to get to know each other more intimately one morning when we were left at the house alone together. Sylvie had told me of some standing stone dolmens very close in the area. She wanted to take me there. We hopped in her car and we were off, driving down a one-lane winding road, praying not to meet another car.

We came to the village Montardier where a large castle hovered above the village. We passed by a large stone Madonna that was the centerpiece of the town. Her face had blackened over many years of exposure to the elements. She was a Black Madonna that nature claimed.

Not far from the village the landscape began to change. We came to an open rocky field, the perfect place to find wild lavender, thyme and rose bushes full of rosehips that were ripening in the late summer sun.

We were looking for the cross road where the stone dolmen temple of the ancient Gauls was supposed to be. There was a small sign and before we knew it we were in front of the entrance of a rock chamber as if cut from the Earth. I checked the landscape for the Ley-Line energies and I found a low ridge on the horizon line with a dragon's head curled up half way down the hill. The other side of the road also had a second ridge that I assumed also was a dragon line but there were to many barbwire fences between me and the ridge to make a full investigation. We bowed our heads low and crawled in the earthen chamber and took our place on the dirt floor. I opened my backpack to take out a small silver flask of wine and poured the liquid into a miniature silver chalice. I put the wine to my lips and began to pray.

O eau benie	Blessings to the God of the Water.
Je te voit	I see you and I thank you.
Je te remercie	
O terre benie	Blessings to the God of the Earth.
Je te voit	I see you and I thank you.
Je te remercie	
O air benie	Blessings to the God of the Air.
Je te voit	I see you and I thank you.
Je te remercie	
O feu beni	Blessings to the God of Fire.
Je te voit	I see you and I thank you.
Je te remercie	
O dragon benie	Blessings to the Dragon God.
Je te voit	I see you and I thank you.
Je te remercie	

I poured the wine onto the earth for each invocation. Then I took a sip of wine and handed the chalice to Sylvie. Sylvie then also addressed the elements in her own prayers in perfect French. I then took out my little bag that was filled with little rose buds and we began to offer roses between the cracks of the stone walls.

Sylvie sang a beautiful chant to the earth and we got up from our knees and re-entered the world.

Sylvie mentioned to me the God Belen, the Great God of the Gauls. Belen had a wife, sister whose name was Belisama. Belisama was a virgin who was impregnated with the spirit of Belen. They had a divine child whose name was Gargantua, meaning Son of the Great Stone.

Gargantua one day mounted Belen's horse and traveled east to west. He followed the movements of the seasons. Gargantua involved himself with the fertility of the land, the moving of giant stones and creating oak forest, fishponds and lakes. Many towns still hold the name of Belen such as Belegaard, Belengarde, Blenes, Balin and Beneau to name a few.

I looked to the side of the road and there it was, a mini Stonehenge. It was amazing, a circle of stones in an open field between two Ley-Lines, gently curving with the natural landscape. Just about the time we got out of the car a dragon cloud formed over the hill and I understood we were on the dragon line. This was a way the dragon spirits confirmed my findings.

Sylvie and I crawled under a barbed wire fence and before you knew it we were at the gateway of the circle.

Each stone had its own peculiar shape. Some looked like guardians. Another very dark stone looked like a Madonna and child. There was a dolmen in the middle. Sylvie explained that this circle was a calendar that marked the changing of the seasons.

I quickly brought out my bag of rosebuds and we offered to the stones of the gateway. We then entered the circle going directly to the center dolmen. We made our offerings of wine and rosebuds. When my silver chalice hit the center stone it made a perfect bell like tone. Sylvie went in one direction of the circle and I went the other direction, offering each stone a rose and a prayer. As I walked around the circle I also offered each stone the sound of my silver chalice. The sound of silver hitting rock created a pure tone most pleasing to the ear. Somehow in the process my finger was cut and the next stone I offered to also received some blood that ran from my finger. I wondered if some ancient blood rites had taken place in the circle and the spirits of the place wanted a little blood offering since it was a self-arising event.

Sylvie and I met at the gateways and walked back into the center. Sylvie leaned against the center dolmen and began to create sounds that came from a very deep part of her; I held the space for her. She sang the primordial song of her own experience. She was connected to the earth and also her own soul. I sat squatting on the earth, hands folded in prayer and holding the silence for the unfolding event of her expression. She completed and we walked through the circle, gathering lavender and thyme, making little memory bouquets recording the day's events.

Pezenas

Andreas and I just have been traveling through the area of Béziers to go on a pilgrimage to the small village of Pezenas-Herault. We were searching the Black Madonna Notre Dame de Bethléem. We arrived in the ancient village that had once been dedicated to the Roman god Heraclia.

We walked through the village streets, looking for the central church of the village. We found the church, but upon our entry, we realized it was not the home of the Black Madonna. But the church had a sacred art exposition, which we then attended.

Inside we saw many sacred objects. I stood before the relics of Joan of Arc, St. Theresa of Avila and St. Theresa, the little rose. I bathed in the spiritual presence of these sacred relics, which contained the hair or bones of each saint.

But what intrigued me, were two beautifully carved wooden spiral columns. This type of column is often found in the village churches of France. As I have mentioned before in my writings, these columns are used in sacred architecture as the conductors of the Ley-Line energies. The magnetic currents from the earth are directed upward though the columns which run up the walls of the church. The energy travels into the church steeple that spirals into the heavens. This makes the church a place where heaven and earth meet. These particular wooden columns were decorated with carvings of grapes growing on the vine. You might remember that Christ referred to grapes in many of his parables.

Looking at these columns made me reflect about all the vineyards we had traveled to in France. Southern France is rich with Ley-Line energies. Between these sacred energies there exists fertile earth filled with vineyards. I began to understand how the subtle Wouivre system worked through the grape vines. The spirits of the Nagas live in the water. When you look closely at the vines of the grapes, you can see the serpentine energy expressing itself with every twist and turn of the vine. The fruit of the vine is made into wine and wine is the blood of the land. The vines are the veins of the black virgin herself.

Wine was a sacred sacrament in ancient European cultures, even before the time of Christ. Jesus was an initiate of these ancient mysteries and when he raised his cup at the last supper, he said, "This is my blood." He also took the bread and said, "This is my body." He asked us to do this in his remembrance. Why did he say this? Christ knew who he was. He was anchored in the Presence of his own Immortality. He fully realized that this ever-changing world of matter, which includes our bodies and our genetical conditioning (the blood), is only temporary.

Christ was asking us through the sacred sacrament to remember who we are beyond the world of matter. We can remember the power of the sacred sacrament of wine the next time we are around a dinner table with friends. The simple act of going around the table and saying blessings with each sip of wine creates a sacred circle of well-wishing for everyone at the table.

The wine toast is a form of this ritual. But rather than doing one or two toasts, each person prays on each sip of wine. You might be surprised what can happen to a dinner party when this takes place at a table.

We moved through the village of Pezenas to find the church of Saint Ursula, where the Black Madonna resided. We walked through Saturday's vegetable market and turned down a narrow street and found the church. We walked in to find an old woman who greeted us and she pointed the way to the Vierge Noir.

I knelt down on a marble slab that was in front of the chapel of the Virgin. She was magnificent. She was black as coal and dressed in garments of gold. You could truly feel the power of the icon and the centuries of prayers that had been offered in this holy place. There were local women of the village who were dedicated to caring for the Black Virgin. They realized the power of this icon and had cultivated their own prayer power through years of dedication. I saw one woman from the village, then another, and another, offering their prayers. Then afterwards they chatted in the back of the church. It was as busy as a sewing bee.

This black virgin has existed since 1311. She arrived alone on a boat in the harbor of Bologne. It was purchased by the Knights of St. John and brought to this church of St. Ursula.

This icon was known for its miracles of protection in the epidemics of 1852-1854. It also delivered protection against drought for 7 years around 1840. It protected the area while other surrounding areas were affected.

I began to enter deep into meditation as I knelt before the Virgin. There are many different meditation postures in the East. I find kneeling is also a particular posture to receive the energies of a sacred place. Your knees are in contact with the ground and the posture of the body is straight. So the energy flows freely through the body. The marble slab under my knees gave me a good connection with the foundation of this sacred ground.

The radiance of Notre Dame was golden. The more I stared at her, the more the Golden Light unfolded around her as her inner essence revealed itself to me in vision. The darkness of her skin felt completely connected to the deep secrets of fertility that lay beneath the earth.

It was like being in the Presence of the Earth Goddess, in her full power and splendor. It was absolutely electrifying. She was like the concentrated power of the mountains, the vineyards, the fields of lavender and the groves of olives. I was awe-struck. The silence arose. My body stiffened as the sacred also ran through me. My head bent back from the force of the energy I was experiencing. No thought. No mind. There was just the unfolding presence of experience. Tears began to roll down my cheeks for the Blessings I was receiving. She was Grace.

I felt the prayers of the old caretaker joining and weaving together with our prayers.

I began to pray for all the ones I loved, for all the ones I knew and had met along my way. More and more faces of people came into my consciousness. I realized when I am in such Grace, it is a good time to remember others and place their needs at the feet of this healing Virgin.

She was Black Isis. She was the Earth Mother. She was the Ancient Voice of Wisdom that can only be cultivated through experiencing life.

She was the Sacred Marriage of Christ in the very atoms of matter. She offers an invitation of this great wedding feast on the altar of your own heart, letting the matter of your own physical form become a living vessel for consciousness. I felt her secrets.

The Land of the Cathars
Béziers

Béziers is at the edge of Cathar land. The Cathars were a group of Gnostics that lived in France in the medieval ages. They called their faith the 'Church of Love.' It emphasized the direct experience with the Divine, rather than relying on the written word from the Bible. This approach placed them in confrontation with the Catholic Church. The European inquisition started with the Albiginsian Crusade. The sole purpose of this crusade was to annihilate Catharism in France and the Catholic Church was very successful in that endeavor.

The area where the greatest Cathar families lived was between Argues and Rennes-le-Château. This area was our destination. The two most famous Black Virgins in the area were Notre Dame de Paix (now located in Paris) and Notre Dame de Marseille, which is located close to the small town of Limoux.

We arrived in Béziers, where our friend met us at the train station. She drove us to her family's beach house, located directly at the Mediterranean Sea in Valros. In our room the windows were constantly open. We could smell the salty air and hear the sound of the rolling waves, which became the lullaby that sent us to sleep each night.

In the afternoon we went to the center of Valros. We dropped Andreas off at the local Internet Café and my girlfriend showed me more of this beach town.

She did not speak any English and my French is limited, but we both understood and spoke fluently the language of the heart, where all barriers are broken. This is where we met.

We visited the local church, a rather modern building for France, since most churches here are at least 300 or more years old. We walked through the door; not a soul was in the pews. Far in the corner, hidden among the bigger statues, there was a small Black Virgin. This is where our pilgrimage begun into the land of the Cathars.

We both lit red votive candles and placed them before the Vierge Noir and sat down on those familiar, hard wooden pews. We closed our eyes and went into deep meditation.

As I circled Kriyas through my body, the name of Jesus Christ arose in my mind and I began repeating the sound of 'Jesus' with my inhalation and 'Christ' with my exhalation. My consciousness was traveling the 'thornless rose path' with each Kriya.

Limoux

We were traveling the freeway towards Limoux. We could see the ancient Cathar castles dotting the landscape. At one point we drove by a very large castle that was big enough to hold and surround an entire village. This was near the town of Carcassone, close to Limoux.

The church of Notre Dame de Marseille was outside the town of Limoux. With a little help from the locals, we finally arrived in front of the church door. The door of the church was ancient and weathered by time. Above the threshold it was adorned with symbols that represented the womb of Mary. A beautiful wooden virgin was painted in hues of blue and coral, as it stood guarding the door.

Andreas then began telling the story of seeing this Black Virgin for the first time in 1993. He has never been exposed to, nor understood the meaning of, the Black Virgin. However, his experience was so profound that he realized these icons represent important portals of consciousness.

He went on to explain that they were gateways to the experience of Samadhi if one could meditate in front of such a statue long enough. This was his own experience meditating with the virgin of Limoux

We walked into the church that was in the process of being remodeled. Since it was lunchtime, one of the most important hours in France, the workers were leaving. One thing you can depend on in France: the long lunch breaks. So we knew we would have plenty of time for meditation.

There she was at the side of the church. But unfortunately she was behind a brass grill. So it was hard to see her without putting the face close to the grill. Many of the ancient Black Virgins in these remote chapels began to be subjected to theft, beginning in the 1980s. The churches, in order to protect their sacred objects, had to lock away their icons. This was also the case here in Limoux. This Vierge Noir was made of hard wood, but her face was light brown, rather than black. We called her La Vierge Du Chocolate. The cult of the Madonna of Limoux began at 1011 and she

196

became a major pilgrimage site by 1380. She was known to heal the blind and also livestock. We also found a spring next to this church that followed the Ley-Line system. This spring had a sign above it that said, *The Water Which Heals 1000 Evils.* There were many marble plaques that testified to the many miraculous healings that had taken place.

Just like La Reine du Paix of Paris, the Virgin of Limoux was connected with the Merovingian bloodline. This area became a refuge center for the Merovingian families after the murder of Dagobert II, a king of the Merovingians. The Merovingians recognized the Goddess Isis. Some of these royal lineages had been buried in St. Germain in Paris, which was once an ancient temple of Isis. St. Germain is the oldest known church in Paris.

The Merovingian King Childebert I brought back treasures from Solomon's Temple in the Holy Land. The Psalms of Solomon, wherein Solomon poetically speaks of his Sacred Marriage with the Queen of Sheba. (She is black but she is beautiful.) Some of the Black Virgins were brought into France from such pilgrimages.

The Merovingian King Dagobert II was born in 656 and he was raised in the Monastery of Slane in Ireland. He had married a Celtic Princess who later died. His second wife was Giselle de Razes, whose home was Rennes-le-Château. This marriage arrangement brought Dagobert back to France to claim his right to the throne.

In December 23 of the year 676 he went hunting in the Forest of Woëvre. He was resting his back against a tree, when his own godson stabbed him in the eye, under the orders Pepin of Heristal. This brought to an end the line of the Merovingian Kings. Dagobert was declared a saint 200 years later. His feast day is December 23. Saint Dagobert is often seen in icon art depicted with a wolf. The Merovingian Kings believed that Mary Magdalene and Christ was part of their ancestry.

The Land of the Cathars is laced with the history of the Merovingian lineage. The Cathars themselves believed in the marriage of Mary Magdalene and Christ. Their religious purity reflected the spirituality of the Essenes in the Holy Land. Christ's family was part of the Essenes.

We all settled down for meditation in the chapel. This virgin's eyes were wide open and she had a tranquil smile on her face. She was crafted in a doll-like style. Because of her exceptionally large eyes, people believed in her power to heal blindness.

I finished my meditation and headed down a trail that went to a dry riverbank. As I went back up the trail, I found the miraculous spring that cures the 1000 evils. A sign said in French that the water could be used but not for drinking. Soon our little party gathered around the spring and we began to pray spontaneously. We took turns washing ourselves with the water and filling our bottles.

We slowly walked back towards the church, filled with the spirit of the water. Then we found a picnic table among twisted, weathered pine trees and ate our lunch.

The Chair of Isis

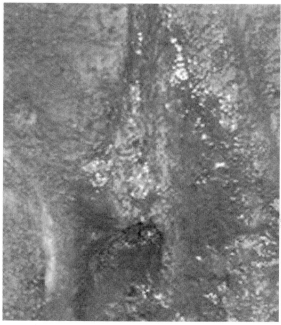

We finished our picnic and pushed onward to Rennes-les-Bains, which translates into 'The Bath of the Queens'.

We drove through old, winding roads. As we took the turn-off into the direction of Rennes-les-Bains, I noticed that the landscape started changing. Large rock ridges loomed over the road. I asked my friend to stop the car, for I sensed that I could find the dragon guardians within these ridges. This was a holy place, where ancient dragons serpentined through the landscape, holding secret powers that lay deeply hidden in the land. I found the head of the dragon. I searched for the second dragon-line that I knew had to be hiding near-by.

I recorded my findings with my trusty digital camera and we continued down the road. We arrived at Rennes-les-Bains. This village is famous for its spas and natural mineral springs.

My girlfriend Christy from California had told me stories about this area a few years ago. It had been one of her favorite places when she visited France. She conveyed to me about a place that had stone carved as a chair, called the seat of Isis

It took a bit of asking where this place was, because it had been renamed 'The Devil's Chair' (La Chaise du Diable). This type of name changing often happened to many sites in nature where one could commune with the natural powers of the land. To discourage such heathen activities, the

good Christians of the community would rename the place. We made a few wrong turns and then we finally came to the path to the Seat of Isis. It was hot and a steep climb but we finally arrived in a cool forest.

There was a clearing where a large rock had been shaped into a chair. What I found interesting was that next to the Chair was a natural mineral spring. The spring water was gathered in several basins.
However, it was the spring itself that had a peculiar shape. The water trickled out of a hole in the ground that looked like a woman's vagina. The Goddess was revealing her most sacred parts in the quiet clearing of this forest.

The water itself was filled with iron and minerals. I could tell by the red-colored deposits around the opening in the earth.

This was water that could bring strength, I told my girlfriend and we began to apply the water to our faces. We took long and deep sips from the spring to cool ourselves from the climb up the hill.

We took turns sitting in the chair of Isis. It was a beautiful moment. To find the seat of Isis that is hidden in the forest outside of Rennes-le-Bains go to the village's map that is posted in the public parking lot at he beginning of the village. It will be listed on the map as Devil's Chair. But its original name is the chair of Isis.

La Source de la Magdala

We were told about another spring in the Rennes-les-Bains area: La source de la Magdala. We drove a short way out of town and saw a small sign that pointed to the site. We piled out of the car and started walking along a path into the forest.

We came across the stream. The source of the Magdala was on the other site. It was hot and before I even got close to the spring, I was bathing in the cooling water. I was so happy being in the stream, among the luscious ferns and the smooth river rocks.

The source of the Magdala was made up of many small springs in the same area. I found that there was a clay deposit next to the spring under debris of leaves. I began to dig away through the leaves and soon I reached soft gray clay. I immediately dug out handfuls of clay and handed it over to Andreas. I wrapped up a glob of clay in several leaves to take with me for later use. Then we walked a few yards to the left and found another spring. There water was bubbling from the earth from a yoni-shaped mound of the Goddess. It was amazing that both the spring of Isis and Magdalene looked both alike.

Over the last 17 years new light has been shed on the saga of Jesus and Mary Magdalene. Some of these sources of new information have connected Christ and Magdalene with the older Egyptian initiations of Isis and Osiris. It seem that some of the people here in southern France have understood this connection for a long time.

The Black Madonnas represent remnants of the influences of the Dark Egyptian Goddess Isis. I believe that Mary Magdalene also understood the Dark Goddess archetype and brought it here to southern France.

A few days later, I took the clay I had gathered and fashioned an image of the Goddess that I dried in the heat of the Mediterranean sun.

Directions to this area:
http://en.wikipedia.org/wiki/Rennes-le-Château

Mont Bugarach and Rennes-le-Château

We continued on our pilgrimage and entered an area that was Ley-Line land par excellence. Dragon ridges were everywhere and the atmosphere felt uplifting. As we turned the corner, there was Mont Bugarach.

Some of the French people involved in the world of consciousness compare Mont Bugarach with Mount Shasta even though the two Mountains do not at all look alike. There is a very high vibration that could be felt in the presence of Bugarach that reminds me of Mount Shasta. Everyone in the car became very excited by the energy that we started to experience.

It was afternoon as we approached Rennes-le-Château. Over time a lot of material has been written about the small village here in southern France. Rennes-le-Château was the ancient capital of the Visigoths of this region. It was also a center of the cult of Mary Magdalene. The church of Rennes-le-Château was dedicated to Mary Magdalene in 1059. During that time, Catharism experienced a climax of strength and influence in that area. Sigebert IV and Merovi Levi of the Merovingian bloodline found refuge in Rennes-le-Château with Visigothic relatives on January 17, 681. This is a place where legend, myth and reality all mingle together.

Some people seem to believe that Rennes-le-Château held hidden secrets concerning the marriage of Christ and Mary Magdalene.

To find the truth behind the many veils of layered history is up to each individual. There is no concrete evidence that Christ and Mary Magdalene were married and had a child. There are theories that support the possibility that this child then would have been the beginning of the Merovingian bloodline.

We must take into consideration, though, that the Catholic Church went through great efforts to stamp out any influence that did not support their dogma. That dogma changed dramatically the course of *recorded* history.

One of the big problems with history is that it is written by individuals whose personal projections color the story in accordance with their own filter of reality. I see this even today as the Western feminists project their own interpretations of who Mary Magdalene was.

You can see the interpretations of Christ in the many different expressions of Christianity. For example, the Christ in a Baptist Church appears to be very different than the Christ in a Catholic mass. We must all remember this while we research the new mysteries of the life of Mary Magdalene, Christ or any other archetype. The true focus of this research should be to connect with the truth behind the archetype. That truth is found through direct experience in the inner chambers of one's soul. This is the place where opinions and projections of the archetypes dissolve. We then can experience the essence of these spiritual giants. According to the true spirit of the Cathars, this is found in the silence of God. A mystery can only be hinted at. The unspoken is left to the experience of the individual.

These sacred pilgrimage sites are filled with symbols that give us clues of what might have taken place. But it is when one stops and meditates in the radiance of such sites that we are touched by essence.

The Spirit of Christ can unfold in our minds and thoughts. Worries and hopelessness will then fall away. That spirit of Christ lives in each one of us. If we find ourselves in a female form, we become Christ's Magdalene; we become Christ's beloved. If we find ourselves in a male form, we become a radiant sunrise within our own heart. This is the closest we can get to the truth of all the stories.

We entered the chapel of Rennes-le-Chateaus, which was filled with many tourists, snapping pictures, looking for their own truth of the situation.

I closed my eyes, went into meditation and smiled. We are all longing. We are all looking – each in our own way. That longing is a close as our own heartbeat.

We walked through the streets of the Village. I viewed the landscape from the tower of the Magdalene. Mazes of Ley-Lines wove through the environment, manifesting the power of the Creator's hand and the beauty found in the body of Mother Earth.

Directions: Rennes-le-Château
http://www.rennes-le-chateau.org/rlctoday/eng-trajet.asp
Directions: Mt Bugarach: go to Google Map 11190 Mt. Bugarach

Les Gorges d'Heric

Madonna Rock with Child

It was July 22, the feast of Mary Magdalene. We decided to travel to the Montagnes Noires, the Black Mountains of Southern France. My friends had packed a picnic lunch and we drove to an outing in Nature. We came into the area Les Gorges D'Ileric that was filled with many strange rock formations. The rocks hung high over the hiking trail that ran alongside a crystal blue river.

It was a hot summer day and we began to walk up the trail. There were signs along the road that explained many of the myths and legends that are connected to this unusual area. The rock formations appeared to take the shapes of the Gods and Goddesses of Nature.

One rock formation took the shape of a Goddess with long massive hair that fell down her back. I saw the Naga spirit of La Reine Melusine, the Goddess that has a serpent tail. She hovered above the rushing river, revealing her shape in many different colored layers of stone.

But what surprised was a massive rock image that appeared as a Mesolithic Black Madonna holding a baby wrapped in swaddling clothes. I remembered the story of the Gauls, of the Goddess Belisama who gave birth to Gargantua. As I stared at this black rock image of the Madonna I realized how the ancient Gauls could come up with such legends. This sacred area represented the crystallization of the Deities of Nature and they were everywhere, watching over us as we slowly walked up the trail.

Child in Rock

We finished our hike, returned to the road and continued traveling through small mountain villages. The Tour de France, the world-famous bicycle race, had just traveled through the same villages a few days before.

The windy mountain roads led us to a rich valley below that was filled with green vineyards. The unripe grapes were heavy on the vine, which held the promise of a rich harvest.

Monastère de Soncade

We arrived at the Monastère de Soncade, which was completely surrounded by vineyards. I realized this monastery was on the Wouivre system since one of the monks told us about a Menhir stone in the vineyard.

We paid a small fee to enter the monastery tour and we walked through the door of their chapel. There she was, a beautiful medieval icon of Mary Magdalene. I was so happy to see this image on the feast day of the Magdalene.

This monastery was no ordinary Catholic establishment. The Templar Cross was on every wall of the Chapel. But there were also large wooden staffs used as candleholders in the corner of this room, which also was marked with the signs of the Templars. There was meditation energy here and you could feel spiritual adepts had charged this Sacred Space.

But it was the Baptism fount that made me look twice. A huge copper cauldron decorated with Celtic knot work began expressed the deeper secrets of the monks that were practicing in this monastery. Copper is the metal of the Goddess Venus and the cauldron is the ancient symbol for the womb of the Goddess. But above the cauldron was a copper staff with the head of a stag. The Stag King is the consort of the Ancient Goddess. When the Stag King magically mates with the Goddess of the land, the blessing of fertility is spread though the fields. This Baptism Fount was not ancient. It was new and created with these symbols with purpose.

When I began to walk out of the Chapel, my friend spoke to one of the monks, introducing me as a writer and researcher of the Black Madonna. The monk looked at me with a knowing eye and began to tell me about how the Black Madonna was influenced by the Goddess Isis.

When we walked away, I felt like I had met a man who had tapped into the ancient Spirit of the Knights Templar, who embodied the true understanding of the Magdalene and who had remembered the secrets.

Daurade Basilica in Toulouse

We were in Toulouse on our way to see the Black Virgin that is housed in the Daurade Basilica. Toulouse is a beautiful city that once was a part of the Roman Empire. The Basilica was built over the Temple of Apollo the Roman Sun God.

The ancient Sun Wheel with 12 spokes originally inspired the *Croix du Languedoc*, which is the emblem of Toulouse. The emblem of Toulouse can now be found in the center of Place du Capitole designed by Raymond Moretti.

There are legends about this sacred spot that go way back into Roman history. The Roman Consul Cepio in the year 109 B.C. drained a lake where the Basilica now stands. He was looking for the Gold of Toulouse. This was a stolen treasure taken by the Gauls at Delphi. The word Delphi comes from the word Delphus, which means womb. They did not find the gold, but what they did find was an icon of the Pallas Athena.

The Basilica was going through reconstruction in 1760 and workers found a statue of Aphrodite inside one of the walls. Another gift left behind by the Romans

Toulouse was the city that started the Albigensian Crusade. This crusade was the beginning of the Inquisition. The Cathars were gnostics that believed that direct experience with God was more important than the written word. This belief was against the Law of the Roman Catholic Church. The Lords of Northern France fought in the Albigensian Crusades. They wanted the rich lands and castles of the Cathars. The Church and the Lords of the North together went forth to the province of Languedoc and killed and burned men, women and children in the name of God. Religious crusades became profitable both for Church and state.

The Cathars believed in the teachings of Christ. They also recognized Mary Magdalene and honored the Roman goddess Minerva (Athena in Greece). In 1210 the Cathar Castle of Minerva was burned and 180 people died.

The Daurade Basilica was also the chapel of the Visigothic Kings of Toulouse. During the 11th century it became the church of the troubadours and a center for the *Jeux Floraux,* which were the floral games in May. These games honored the Black Virgin. During this time Toulouse became one of the greatest courts in Europe. The troubadour tradition brought to life poetry, music, chivalry, and courtly love. They emphasized intellectual and metaphysical thought. The troubadour's influence began in 1100 and started to decline in the 14th century with the coming of the Black Plague.

When we entered the church I found it weighed heavy with the tradition and the history of the past. But as we approached the Black Virgin shrine I felt I had come to the womb of the sacred. You would not know that the Black Virgin and Child is only a bust since they are adorned under beautiful handmade garments. They were enshrined in a mosaic altar.

I sat close to the altar and below my feet was a mosaic tile serpent. This was the church symbol of the snake that tempted Eve. But for me this symbol held deeper mysteries to behold.

The great river Garonne was right outside of the Virgin's Basilica. The serpent is an ancient symbol of rivers and waters. The Garonne River is 575 km long and is used today for inland shipping. The word Garonne comes from the word Garumna in the old language of Aquitania. This word means stone and source (onna).

Our Lady of Good Birth, the Black Virgin of Daurade, was once a major pilgrimage place for pregnant women. Prayers to this Virgin would ensure a safe birth. But she also was known for a miracle in 1637 when the plague was beginning to invade the city. They brought the statue down from the altar and walked through the streets. Shortly after the procession the plague stopped.

Unfortunately the Black Virgin of Daurade is a replacement of a Black Virgin that was destroyed in 1799 during the French Revolution. But I feel this Black Virgin still holds the power to answer ones prayers.

Today not every woman wants to have a child. But we can still pray to the Black Virgin to help us birth our spiritual self, our dreams and our noble projects. We can give birth in many different ways. We can also pray to the Black Virgin to heal our own childhood birth traumas so that we can easily manifest in this world. I feel Our Lady of Good Birth can answer our prayers in many different ways.

Directions: 1 Rue de la Daurade
31000 Toulouse,
05 61 21 38 32

Other churches you might like to visit in Toulouse:

Cathedral St Etienne
Place de St. Etienne
31000, Toulouse
Built in the 11th century in Romanesque style

Notre Dame du Taur
12 Rue du Taur
31000, Toulouse
Gothic architecture

Convent of Jacobin
Parvis des Jacobin
Enter from Rue Lakanal
This is the monastery of the Dominicans who were part of the Cathar Inquisition.

Basilica St. Sernin
Place St. Sernin
31000 Toulouse
This Basilica is the largest Romanesque church in the world.

The Black Stone of Agde Hérault

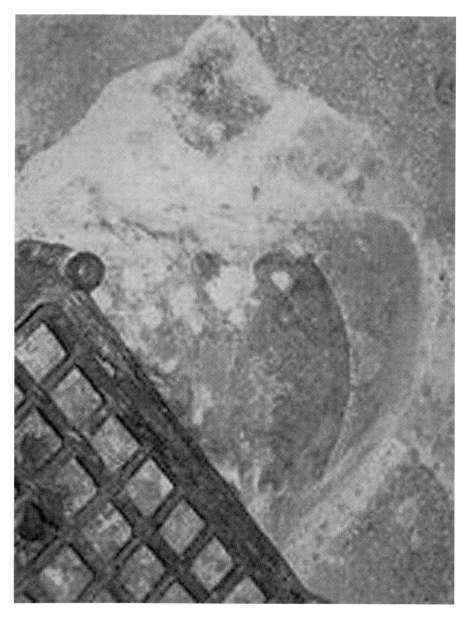

We went to the coastal town of Agde-Hérault in search of a church that held a miraculous black stone with the impression of the virgin.

We arrived at the beach of the town where the surf was wild and waves were beating the shoreline. Two lighthouses stood together on a small cape. We were looking for the chapel of Notre-Dame-de-la-Genouillade and finally found it. It had an outside altar. This altar seemed more befitting for an ancient pagan rite than belonging into a Catholic church.

Strange trees grew around the area. They resembled Dryad Goddesses, guarding the stone altar. This natural temple was in the center of the church parking lot. However, this was not what we were looking for. There were two churches. After asking for the whereabouts of the Madonna Stone, we entered the smaller chapel on the church ground. There in the middle of the floor was a shrine, created in the earth. And there was a large, black stone that was protected by an iron grill. This rock carried the impression of the knee print of the Virgin. It was acclaimed that her appearance on the rock saved the town from a tidal wave.

Red votive candles were placed on the black stone. As I closely observed the stone, I actually could see the head of a Madonna within the rock.

Phoenicians settled the town 2,500 years ago. The town was named after the good Goddess Agatha. This black stone Madonna echoes the ancient worship of the Goddess Sybil, who was originally worshipped as a black stone.

The image of the Virgin who knelt upon the black volcanic rock and stopped the overwhelming forces of nature made me reflect. The tidal wave is like our emotions that wash through the dramas of our lives. It can bring destruction to the very fabric of what we hold dear and near.

We all have experienced destructive events in our lives, caused by our own overwhelming emotions. To master the forces of the many human emotions, sometimes it seems to require a miracle. The miracle that needs to occur is to quiet our minds before we get drawn into the cycle of action and reaction. When we experience the emotions of fear, anger and even depression, we can realize that these emotions are connected to our thought processes.

The human mind, when left to its own devices, can run away like a pack of wild horses. Especially, when motivated by very negative emotions. We need to simply slow down and stop. When we breathe deeply in through our nose and out through the mouth, we can begin to release the emotions that actually can change the state of your mind. This sounds very simple. However, being in the midst of one's emotions, it requires mindfulness to remember.

When we use this little breathing technique for perhaps 20 minutes it will calm the emotions. Once the emotions are calm, we can begin to witness the roots of the emotional behavior.

This is a good way to stop the tidal waves in our lives and reflect in the tranquil mirror of equanimity.

Directions: Agde Hérault
http://www.multimap.com/world/FR/Languedoc-Roussillon/H%C3%A9rault/Agde

Afterword

My travels through France have deepened my own understand of myself. This is the purpose all of True Pilgrimage. It has been a privilege to have this life opportunity to experience such places. I want to thank each person who personally made it possible for me to see these sacred sites; people who opened their hearts and their homes to me and took the effort to bring me to the Sacred Sites so this book could be written. I especially want to thank Andreas Mamet for his devoted work to the editing process of this manuscript. I would like to thank Olivier Vinet Olivier Bourillot and Albine Pepino for taking me to so many churches. I offer a deep thank you to Mary Theresa and Patrick for taking me into the land of the Cathars. I would like to thank Alok Hsu Kwang for inviting me to Egypt which deepened my insights into the Goddess Isis which help bring a completion to this work.

January of 2014 my mother Noreen Abbott died. A few days after her death my family gathered to celebrate her life. My son Joshua had been studying my father's family's genealogy which goes back to the third century of Europe. A few years before a professional genealogist had also study my father's family lineage. She had told me at the time how interesting my father's lineage was. The day of my mother's wake I looked at my father's lineage and discovered that our family line can be traced back to the Merovingian Kings of France going into both Dagobert I and Dagpbert II, King Clovis and King Childebert. I am there great great and many more great granddaughter I did not realize this when I was writing this book or visiting many of the sacred sites of my ancestors. The Merovingian Kings claimed to be from the direct bloodline of Mary Magdalene and Christ. The Merovingian Kings help establish the devotion to the Black Virgins in France.

May the truth of these places ring free and be liberated from the heavy burden of the past. May the beautiful lands of this country be blessed, protected and understood for the future generations. And may we learn from our history, and be open to people of different religion, different thoughts and different colors. May we be tolerant and loving to each other and caring to this precious Earth.

Raylene Abbott

Author Biography

Raylene Abbott's spiritual training has spanned over the last 40 years. She began her path into Magdala and Black Madonna traditions in 1992, with the meeting of Elizabeth Kelley, a priestess ordained in the Church of Mary Magdalene. This Magdalene lineage comes direct from the South of France since Medieval times. Raylene's path led her living in France for 4 1/2 years teaching meditation. Her passion led her to traveling the pilgrimage route of the Black Madonna and Magdalene.

Raylene is an international author. Her book was published in France in 2006 "L'Emergence de la Femme Divine" {The Emergence of the Divine Woman}. This same book later was published in Italy, Turkey, Japan and the USA as "Between the Visions. Her recent book "A Mystics Journey to the Sacred Sites of France" is newly in paperback. She is a published author of six different books.

This year 2014 Raylene was presented her ancestral genealogy of her Father's lineage and she discovered that her bloodline can be traced back to the Merovingian Kings of France, known as the Rose-line. Her newly found realization was that she had pilgrimaged, made offerings and written about her own ancestors…

Raylene Abbott is available on Facebook. Her email address is
rayleneabbott@gmail.com

Research Resources

The Cult of the Black Virgin by Ean Begg
published in 1985 by Arkana an imprint of Routledge and Kegan Paul Ltd.

The Woman's Myths and Secrets by Barbara G Walker
© 1983 Harpers of San Francisco

The Definitive Guide to the Da Vinci Code Paris Walks
by Peter Caine © 2005
by Orion Books Ltd, London

Eyewitness Travel Guide Paris
Alan Tillier
DK Publishing Inc.

Wikipedia, the free encyclopedia on-line source

The picture below was taken of Gheorghe Chesler. http://www.nightmedia.net/
The pictures of St. Baume and St. Victor's by Olivier Vinet.
All other pictures photographed by Raylene Abbott

Lady of the Ley-Lines